VISCOUNT PALMERSTON, K.G.

VISCOUNT PALMERSTON, K.G.

MARQUIS OF LORNE

NONSUCH

First published 1892
Copyright © in this edition Nonsuch Publishing Limited, 2007

Nonsuch Publishing
Cirencester Road, Chalford, Stroud, Gloucestershire, GL6 8PE, UK
www.nonsuch-publishing.com

Nonsuch Publishing is an imprint of NPI Media Group Limited

British Library Cataloguing in Publication Data
A catalogue record for this book is available from the British Library

ISBN 978-1-84588-381-2

Typesetting and origination by NPI Media Group
Printed in Great Britain

Contents

Introduction to the
Modern Edition

VISCOUNT PALMERSTON (1784–1865) BECAME Prime Minister of the
United Kingdom for the first time in 1855 at the age of seventy-one,
making him the oldest premier in history at the time of first forming a
government. With the exception of one year spent out of office—during
which he helped to form the Liberal Party—he retained the position from
then until his death. This appointment was the culmination of a lifetime
spent in ministerial office, beginning with his appointment as a Junior
Lord of the Admiralty in 1807. His legacy, however, is one characterised
more by his involvement in foreign affairs than his premierships, and he is
best remembered for his manoeuvring of foreign policy through a period
when Britain was at the height of its power.

The majority of Palmerston's ministerial career saw him at the centre
of foreign affairs not only in Europe but also as far afield as south-eatern
Europe, the Middle East and Asia, making him a truly global statesman.
His time at the Foreign Office is characterised by an aggressive, often
misunderstood, policy, which was calculated to strengthen the superiority of Britain and maintain the balance of power throughout Europe. In
essence, Palmerston aimed to pursue preventative methods that would
achieve peace rather than provoke war—policies that could not have
been unpopular in principle. However, his abrasive style, earning him the
nickname 'Lord Pumicestone', and his 'gunboat diplomacy' approach to
dealing with foreign governments who crossed him, together created a
reputation that was tinged with controversy. He was never one to shirk
from threatening the use of force if it was in the national interest, however

seemingly insignificant, and this almost led to his downfall in 1850 when he mobilised the Royal Navy against Greece in defence of a British subject, much to the infuriation of his opponents at home. He nevertheless recovered from such episodes to continue his political career up until his death at the age of eighty-one.

Palmerston's rise to political prominence began at an early age. Born in Westminster on 20 October 1784, the son of Henry Temple, second Viscount Palmerston, and his second wife Mary Mee, Henry John Temple was educated at home before being sent to Harrow School, followed by Edinburgh University and then St John's, Cambridge. It was here, at the age of twenty-one, that he first fought for a parliamentary seat, although he was unsuccessful. Undeterred by this he later attained a junior lordship of the Admiralty and a seat was found for him in the pocket borough of Newport, on the Isle of Wight. A few months later he delivered his first speech in the House of Commons in defence of the expedition to Copenhagen (justified by reference to the ambitions of Napoleon to seize control of the Danish court), which met with such success that Palmerston was asked to take the position of Chancellor of the Exchequer. This he declined in favour of the less important office of Secretary at War, a post that came without a seat in the cabinet. He remained in this role for the next twenty years, proving his abilities to run a department but without wielding any influence upon the general policy of the Tory cabinets that he served and showing little inclination towards other aspects of government. During this early period he was well known in society circles and led an active social life, courting controversy through his intimate friendship with Lady Cowper, although the pair eventually married in 1839 following the death of her first husband. Palmerston was, nevertheless, a charismatic and popular figure and it is not difficult to see how he went on to forge a successful public life and career.

Palmerston's time spent outside the cabinet and in a junior role was soon to come to an end. During the last phase of Lord Liverpool's administration the cabinet began to split along political lines, with the more liberal wing of the government beginning its ascendancy. George Canning's subsequent premiership saw Palmerston remain as Secretary at War, but now with a cabinet seat. However, this administration's duration was short lived and Palmerston, along with his fellow Canningites, was reluctantly forced to join the Duke of Wellington's new government. The partnership did not last long, and when Palmerston made a speech on foreign policy that attacked Wellington he was clearly angling for post of Foreign Secretary post that he was later to gain under Lord Grey. The intervening time was spent in opposition, despite Wellington's request for him to return to office, something Palmerston would not agree to without Grey. It was here that his party allegiance can be seen clearly to have shifted. From the beginning of Grey's premiership in 1830 foreign affairs were, unsurprisingly, placed in Palmerston's hands. He spent the next decade almost uninterrupted at the Foreign Office, with his great successes including securing the independence of Belgium from France and the Netherlands, supporting constitutionalists in Spain and Portugal and isolating the autocratic powers of Austria, Russia and Prussia. His short spell in opposition was followed by further confident displays of foreign policy, including the 1850 dispute between Don Pacifico and the Greek government and his recognition of the new Bonapartist government in France in 1851. This latter move, executed by him without the authorisation of the Queen or cabinet, proved to be a step too far and he was dismissed.

The steps that were to take Palmerston towards his first premiership were, nevertheless, related to his approach to British foreign policy. Following his dismissal he had taken the post of Home Secretary in Lord Aberdeen's new government, and in this position he managed to avoid the blame apportioned to Aberdeen over the Crimean War, when revelations about military incompetence brought about his downfall. The country inevitably turned to Palmerston as his most obvious successor. He was the man who had proved himself to be a patriotic, rigorous and competent Foreign Secretary—whose bold moves in the past had been met with support from the public, if not the establishment. His first administration was duly formed at the beginning of 1855, and within a year he had brought about a peaceful conclusion in the Crimea, reinforcing his popularity with the public. Palmerston's years in office were to continue to be characterised by foreign affairs, with the usual patterns soon re-emerging as his provocative policy in China was condemned by the Opposition. His determination to maintain the balance of power in Europe remained unshaken, however, and he continued to intervene when small states found themselves under threat of invasion from the greater powers, as well as building British coastal and naval defences against the threat of the French. He could claim some successes which retained public confidence in his administration. During the year he spent out of office between his premierships he helped to form the Liberal Party, and returned to government as prime minister shortly after. In this sense Palmerston was the first Liberal prime minister of Great Britain, although he would have perhaps counted himself more as the leader of the nation than the party. He continued in office until his death in 1865, when he caught a chill and died of the resultant fever at Brocket Hall, Hertfordshire.

Preface

Lᴏʀᴅ Pᴀʟᴍᴇʀsᴛᴏɴ's ʟᴏɴɢ ᴀɴᴅ ʙᴜsʏ life extended over more than eighty years, and for nearly sixty of those years he was almost continuously in office. He left behind him an enormous amount of correspondence, official and private, and considerable manuscript material dealing with his actions and opinions. This being so, in the preparation of this brief life the plan has been deliberately chosen of allowing him to speak, wherever this could be done, and thus indicate in his own way, at all prominent points in his career, the objects and motives that influenced him. At the same time, it must be borne in mind that he lived too near the present time to allow of the publication of much that he wrote. Although it is undesirable to repeat what has been already so well told by Lord Dalling and Mr Evelyn Ashley, it has been impossible to avoid occasionally traversing the same ground. Special interest attaches to many quotations in this volume from the fact that the author has had access to a large mass of unpublished material, and some of the letters quoted, and almost all the long comments and criticisms upon public affairs from the pen of Palmerston, appear in print for the first time in these pages.

To show how Lord Palmerston did his duty, what he thought was his duty, and why he thought the line he took should be followed, is the kind of biography he himself would have liked best, and this, within the limits assigned, is what the author has attempted. Palmerston never cared for fulsome adulation, nor would he have desired to be painted either as a saint or a demi-god. He was a 'fair and square' political fighter, who made his way to power when and where he could, but always by above-board work, and always by expressing in public the reasons he gave in private. To bespatter him with flattering epithets would have seemed to his straight-forward and unimaginative temperament misplaced attention and in the worst possible taste—praise absurd in form, as silly in thought.

He would have said to such people, if they desired to praise him for old age and length of office, what his colleague, Wellington, said to a worship-per who, seeing the old Duke about to cross alone the crowded street from the Green Park to Apsley House, begged to be allowed to escort him. After the worshipper had walked with the Duke across to the pavement near the Duke's house, the gentleman who had thus volunteered his company took off his hat to the Field-Marshal, and, with a low bow, expressed his deep sense of the high honour that had been permitted to him, &c. On which the old Duke, standing on the pavement, turned his eagle nose and blue eyes on him, and said only, 'Don't he such a damned fool, sir!"

Sentiment, unless sentiment had sense at its back, had no attraction for these men. They could both govern without 'gush,' or the impulse devoid of prudence which often garnishes the speech of the politician catering to feed the crowd's enthusiasm of the moment. He looked at both sides of a question, and did not hasten to champion one aspect of the matter simply because it had christened itself 'Justice,' or 'Right,' or 'Liberal.' Thus of Ireland he said, '"Tenants' right" is often "landlords' wrong,"' and he sifted down the big words of 'gush' until he got the fine sand of truth. It has been said that genius consists in taking pains, but the saying is of doubtful value. Palmerston was emphatically painstaking, but he was not a genius, whose work may be manifold, but whose career is seldom steady. Genius is more apt to give trouble to others than to take pains itself. Palmerston had a good head, good health which is seldom found with genius, and a matter-of-fact-way of going ahead, making his experience of one matter the solid step from which to judge of the next that came before him. He repeated himself over and over again consistently, in act as well as in phrase—a very ungenius-like quality. A plain Englishman, with many an Englishman's want of the feminine attributes of character, but with most of its best masculine qualities, he plodded on, and finally won that goal of an English statesman's ambition—the honourable, but not always enviable, position of First Minister of the Crown.

Palmerston was, in a sense, fortunate in the period of his life and work. He would in all probability have felt himself strangely out of place in this last decade of the nineteenth century. But with shrewd sagacity he knew how to take fortune at the flood, and if he cannot rank with the greatest of England's Prime Ministers, his career testifies to his own abilities, and also enables us to judge the men and the political forces of the generation to which he belonged.

I

Early Life and Education

Henry John Temple, afterwards Lord Palmerston, was born at Broadlands, the family seat in Hampshire, on October 20, 1784. He sprang from an old family, proud of their descent. He came in direct line from the younger brother of Sir William Temple, the friend of William III, who was Speaker of the Irish House of Commons, and whose son, Henry, was made an Irish peer in 1722. His grandson married a Miss Mee, who belonged to a Gloucestershire family, and who by this marriage became the mother of the future Prime Minister.

In 1795, at the age of eleven, young Henry Temple was sent to Harrow, and when two years had passed, according to the testimony of an old school friend, he had acquired the reputation of being the best-tempered and most plucky boy in the school.

That he was full of life and fun is shown by some extracts from his schoolboy letters to his mother, addressed to Catharine Place, Bath:

'We came down very jolly all the way;' but at an inn there was some mistake about fresh horses, 'and Mr Stanly was in a great passion, and swore at the man, for, by the way, all his horses were out with the lawyers, for the quarter sessions were then on.' This Mr Stanly must have been good ballast, for your H. Temple writes in another letter: 'Mr S. may be very agreeable in a house, but he is very disagreeable to go in a post-chaise with—he sits ten foot broad.' During his school days at Harrow he wrote a letter in Italian and in French in order to show off his accomplishments. 'I hope that brother and sisters all ride out with as much courage as before I left you, and that the black pony has not run away with anybody.' Of an old character about the place he says: 'Dicky Martin, famous for his lies, hobbles about with his stick, and is very attentive to find out new ways of cheating.' He gives many details of the plays he saw when in London during a vacation. 'I wish you would send me two pairs of stumps for cricket, and a good bat. We have accepted the challenge sent us by the Eton boys, who have challenged us to fight, not with cannon and balls, but with bats and balls, eighteen against eighteen.' 'We are going to town to-day to see the King and Queen, and *Fortune's Fool*; I do not know what the pantomime will be. I want a new hat, and new coat and breeches.' 'I got a little cold, which I caught the night I came here by getting up in my sleep, and sitting down upon the foot of my bed, I dare say.' 'I saw the King, Queen, and five Princesses, but as they were in mourning it was not very brilliant; the Queen gives me the idea of a housemaid, and the King is a good-looking man.' It was often remarked in after years that reverence was not a failing of Lord Palmerston's! 'Have you heard the joke of our cannons having made the *Holy* Trinidad more *holy*? I suppose you know that Sir John Jervis is gone after another fleet loaded with dollars to the amount of two or three million.'

There was a strike of which Henry Temple much approved. A half-holiday had been expected and not obtained, 'therefore we all determined not to go into school after dinner, of which the Doctor hearing, threatened if we did not, to expel all the big boys. At last at a meeting it was determined to give the point, and go into school.' 'The boy whom we tossed in a blanket for stealing four shillings has made ample amends for it, having not only paid the boy from whom he stole it, but given him a hare and a pheasant he had sent to him. Lord Althorp is come back with a very bad cold and headache, which he caught going down to the Hove with his Majesty, having been upon deck all night when it blew a heavy gale.' 'A man came here to-day with a nest of hedgehogs in a basket. If I had known where to have put it, I should certainly have bought one to keep Fanny's guinea-pig company, for he must be very solitary.' 'We are both very well in health, tho' not in beauty, Willy's lip being rather swelled by a lick with a ball, and my two blue eyes being exchanged for two black ones in consequence of a battle.' 'Willy' was the brother with whom in later years Lord Palmerston so constantly corresponded.

In those times, perhaps more than at present, it was the custom to send youths to some intermediate place of learning before they entered the English Universities. Brougham, Russell, and Palmerston were sent to Scotland, not to take their chance in lodgings as did other students, but to be placed with Professors of the Universities of Glasgow or Edinburgh. Dugald Stewart had a high reputation, and it was to him at Edinburgh in 1800 that young Palmerston was sent. Stewart was then at the height of his fame, and Henry Temple, as he then was, carefully copied out the professor's lectures. 'In these three years,' he wrote long after, 'I laid the foundation of whatever useful knowledge and habits of mind I possess.' Professor Dugald Stewart's opinion of his pupil is given in a letter dated April 27, 1801: 'With respect to Mr Temple, it is sufficient for me to say that he has completely confirmed all the favourable impressions which I received of him. His talents are uncommonly good, and he does them all possible justice by assiduous application. In point of temper and conduct he is everything his friends could wish. Indeed I cannot say that I have ever seen a more faultless character at his time of life, or one possessed of more amiable disposition.'

To his mother he was always most loving and respectful, repaying the devotion she showed to him in full. On April 17, 1802, his father died, and the lad, who was now in his eighteenth year, succeeded to the family title. His mother addressed a long and solemn letter to him, counselling him as to his future life, advising him to remain at Edinburgh until Professor Dugald Stewart's classes were over, and then to enter Cambridge. There was not one of the wishes expressed by the father in regard to the son's education which was not strictly carried out by his mother. To the wisdom of both parents he was indebted for the excellent start he made in life. He had on his side rank and wealth, but these are often temptations rather than advantages. Luckily for him, the early initiation into political life— far more easily accomplished a century ago than at present—held him by its interests and threw over the early years of his manhood its peculiar spell. It was his mother, too, who led him to visit his Irish estates as soon as possible, and her constant aim was to make her boys truthful, and manly, apt at languages, and diligent in study.

In 1803 Palmerston removed from Edinburgh to St John's, Cambridge, where he remained until 1806, when he was called on to take part in an electoral contest. Two years after he had entered college he lost his mother, of whose loss he spoke with the most bitter sorrow. His own letters and extracts from them will here, as later, be quoted, since the true way to show what a man was is to let him speak for himself. No gloss of his words, no translation of his feelings into the words of a critic or narrator, can be so satisfactory as the quotations of letters describing his own feelings from time to time as events shaped his career. Those written at this time to 'my dear Fanny,' his sister, give us much insight into Lord Palmerston's habits, thoughts, and character while at Cambridge:

'Your pen was so bad you could not even spell with it' … Then after a passage about a horse, and a masquerade: 'I am glad to hear the King is getting better, and I hope he will soon recover entirely, and I dare say you heartily concur with me, both from your loyalty and from your impatience to enjoy the pleasure of being presented … You have now some hopes of breaking your shell, which was rather a forlorn hope, and it would have been a great pity to have provided all your salt-smelling bottles in vain … I hear there is only one objection to the plan of blocking up the Boulogne Harbour, which is that it is wholly impracticable.' He writes a good deal about music, of which he was very fond, and concerts, and the songs that were well sung are always mentioned. Then come in bits on politics. 'I participate very sincerely in the general joy at the minister's exit. How well Ashburton will dance for the next fortnight! I quite envy his partners … I have no doubt that Lord B.'s marriage will be very happy, for I have seldom seen a young lady who was on better terms with herself, and as he will be her better half, perhaps she may transfer some portion of her esteem to him … I began this letter last night, but was too sleepy to finish it, and indeed I make it a rule always to be in bed by one o'clock, as I am regularly up at seven … A friend of mine was in company with one of Fox's intimates the other day, who maintained that Pitt and Fox had always thought alike, and that however they might have differed on particular subjects, they always agreed upon the main principles of government. When his friends hold such language, I think it is pretty evident what Fox's plans are.' A tour with a friend is discussed: 'I think that in five weeks at the utmost we shall be able to see all the southern part of Wales, so, if we set out at the end of June, we shall be at Broadlands at the beginning of August.'

But his mind turns constantly to public affairs: 'What a large proportion of titles there is on the Ministerial list! I thought Canning would come right again,' says this precocious undergraduate, 'and not quarrel with his bread and butter. It never answers. I hear that Bonaparte has offered advantageous terms of peace provided we recognise the Emperorship ... You will no doubt by this time know the cause of the confusion which reigned at Doncaster when we passed through. The Sheffield and Rotherham volunteers received in the morning orders by express to march immediately to Doncaster. The cavalry just entered when we arrived, and an express was sent on to town. A court-martial that was sitting immediately broke up, and the officers ran to the top of the steeple to see Rendlestone Beacon smoking. Nobody knew what the cause of alarm was, but all supposed the French to be landed, but whether at Liverpool, Scarboro', or Harrogate, none could tell. In our mail coach companions we were very lucky. We met with a Colonel Brown, who had served during the whole of the American war, and commanded a large body of Indians—Choctaws, Cherokees, &c ... I suppose you have heard the account of the English prisoners taken by the French and confined at Verdun. They do not seem to be ill off, although indeed their treatment must depend a great deal on the meaning of those *sottises* for which they are liable to be shut up. I hope that making bad puns did not come under that appellation. If so I pity the Johnians who may be there.'

II

Entrance into Public Life

IN 1806 LORD PALMERSTON ENTERED into a contest for the representation in Parliament of the University of Cambridge, and showed the same
dogged determination which he exhibited in all his after-life. In his autobi-
ography he gives the reasons which induced him to take this course, and a
very clear light they throw upon the University life of that day. 'Dr Outram,
my private tutor at Cambridge, more than once observed to me that, as I had
always been in the first class at College examinations, and had been commended for the general regularity of my Conduct, it would not be amiss to
turn my thoughts to standing for the University whenever a vacancy might
happen. My father died in April, 1802, and I lost my mother in January, 1805.
The last misfortune delayed a few months the taking of my degree as Master
of Arts, which it was usual at that time for noblemen to take as an honour,
conferred without examination, at the end of two years after admission. In
January, 1806, Mr Pitt died, and the University had to choose a new member
as well as the King a new minister. I was just of age and had not yet taken my
degree, nevertheless I was advised by my friends at St. John's to stand.'

These reasons, inadequate as they seem now, and as they were felt to be
then, induced Palmerston to offer himself as a candidate for the seat. He
canvassed everyone, and though unknown in comparison with his rivals,
Petty and Althorp, afterwards Lords Lansdowne and Spencer, he made a
good fight, but came in last at the polling.

A curious estimate of Palmerston is expressed by Lord Brougham, in a letter
written to Lord Macaulay, in 1806, in favour of his opponent, Lord H. Petty,
when young Palmerston had made up his mind to stand for Cambridge.

He was certainly young enough to excuse Lord Brougham for misjudging a character that could not have been clearly formed at that time:

'The Government candidate is Lord Palmerston, a young man who only left college a month ago and is devoid of all qualifications for the place. I remember him well at Edinburgh, where he was at college for several years, and what I know of his family and himself increases a hundredfold my wish for Petty's success. The family are enemies to Abolition in a degree that scarcely ever, was exceeded. I presume,' says the foreseeing Brougham, 'that he is so himself. His maxim is that of all the objects of ambition in the world the life of a courtier is the most brilliant. Don't you think that the friends of the cause have the more reason to support Petty the more strenuously?' The future Chancellor made a very bad shot at the character of his Edinburgh fellow-student—the future Prime Minister!

Lord Brougham's letter is remarkable as showing how little known Palmerston was even to his contemporaries, but no opportunity was lost of making himself better known, and after his defeat in the contest of 1806—his first Parliamentary battle—he stood for Cambridge in 1807 and was again beaten; this time by four votes only. 'I did not certainly expect so large a number of voters,' he said, 'and at some future time I may meet with better success.' He had not long to wait, and at the age of twenty-three found himself member of the House of Commons for Newtown, in the Isle of Wight, a constituency controlled by Sir Leonard Holmes. A careful journal was kept by him at this time and at intervals for many years afterwards, and the conditions on which he was nominated by Sir Leonard are mentioned in it. 'One condition was that I would never, even for an election, set foot in the place—so jealous was the patron lest any attempt should be made to get a new interest in the borough.'

Nothing can be clearer or more concise than the account he gives in this journal of the events happening in Europe, and much of it has been published by Lord Dalling, who singles out an observation on Napoleon as showing great sagacity. 'It is a singular circumstance in Buonaparte's political conduct that, so far from concealing his designs, he purposely publishes even the most violent of his projected innovations some time before they are put in execution; and the consequence has uniformly been that, instead of being alarmed and prepared to resist, the world has, by anticipating conquests and changes, become by degrees reconciled to them, and submitted almost without a murmur to the mandates of the tyrant.' He writes of Fox when he died: 'There scarcely ever lived a statesman for whom as an individual the people felt more affection, or in whom as a politician they placed less confidence.' He dissects briefly and with quick penetration the popular movements in politics, and states his views simply and briefly, and with a maturity of thought very striking in one so young.

In 1807, a few months before he secured a seat in the House of Commons for the first time, he was appointed a Junior Lord of the Admiralty by the then Prime Minister, the Duke of Portland. Thus early his interest in foreign affairs was well known to his friends, and he would in the same year have had the refusal of the Under-Secretaryship had it not been accepted by a Mr Bagot, to whom it had been offered before Mr Canning knew of Palmerston's wishes. Nearly a generation, however, was to pass before he took his place at the Foreign Office.

It was not until 1808 that Lord Palmerston delivered his maiden speech. In a letter to his sister he gives his own impression of the performance, one which, as usual, differed considerably from that given by the hearers:

'Admiralty: *Feb.* 4, 1808.—My dear Elizabeth, you will see by this day's paper that I was tempted by some evil spirit to make a fool of myself for the entertainment of the House last night; however, I thought it was a good opportunity of breaking the ice, although one should flounder a little in doing so, as it was impossible to talk any very egregious nonsense upon so good a cause. Canning's speech was one of the most brilliant and convincing I ever heard; it lasted near three hours. He carried the House with him throughout, and I have scarcely ever heard such loud and frequent cheers.'

How others viewed the speech is shown by the following extract from a letter to his brother. The subject of debate was the action of the Government in the expedition against Copenhagen:

'Admiralty: *Feb.* 6, 1808.—Many thanks for your congratulations. I certainly felt glad when the thing was over, though I began to fear I had exposed myself; but my friends were so obliging as to say I had not talked much nonsense, and I began in a few hours afterwards to be reconciled to my fate. The papers have not been very liberal in their allowance of report to me; but the outline of what I said was as follows. In the first place, that the House was, to a certain degree, pledged by the address, in which they expressed their approbation of the expedition; but that the papers were in themselves improper to be produced, as they would betray the sources from whence we obtained intelligence, and expose the authors to Buonaparte's vengeance. That they were unnecessary, because the expedition could be justified without them. That Zealand and the Danish fleet was an object to France; that the neutrality of Denmark would have been no protection, as Buonaparte never did respect neutrality, and was not likely to do so now, when the temptation was the strongest, and his facility the greatest: and that in fact it was evident he did intend to seize the fleet. That Denmark was unable to resist ; but, if she had possessed the means, was unwilling to have exerted them, since it was evident from various circumstances that she had determined to join France.'

'I was about half an hour on my legs; I did not feel so much alarmed as I expected to be. Ever your affectionate brother, PALMERSTON.'

It cannot be said that Palmerston's manner of speaking was particularly good then or at any other time, but there never was any doubt as to what he meant when once the words were pronounced. He often hesitated some time in search of the right word and phrase, and his oratory was never distinguished for any art. It took its strength and secured any effect it produced more because it proceeded from the man than because it was beautiful either in sound of voice or eloquence of expression.

Palmerston always found time amid his work to maintain a lively correspondence with his immediate relatives and friends, and the following extracts from his letters show him in harness, but enjoying to the full the life alike of office and of society. Thus, in writing to his sister while at the Admiralty, he says: 'I am unable to come down to Broadlands, as we are only three at the board, which is the minimum for an official purpose. Our ball last night was very good. We had two quadrilles, which on the whole were tolerably danced. Two of the ladies did very well, the two others but indifferently.' He does get home for a short time, and household details occupy his attention. 'The drawing-room curtains will be applied to mend the chairs and sofas, which are in a state of great decay, and new curtains of sarsnet will be put up, hanging down by the side of the windows in the modern style. The saloon and book-room will have new curtains of the *suppressed* green, with carpets less likely to show stains than the present.

The eating-room curtains will remain for the present; these arrangements will make the house look exceeding smart for the present.' After such a holiday, he says: 'I find all my colleagues glad to have my assistance again.' And then his lifelong dislike of indistinct writing appears. 'The common ink one buys is so dreadfully pale, and yours is of a good deep black.'

'The news of the Portuguese insurrection is not believed, as indeed it was impossible that it could be true, coming as it did from an American captain.' He is keen about maritime rights, and it is curious how in these letters to his kinswomen he plunges from the lightest topic into the most important, giving them his opinions just as he would were he writing to one of his colleagues. 'We have always insisted that the grand principle that neutral bottoms do not make neutral goods should be explicitly recognised, and it was so established in our latest treaties with Russia and Denmark after the last armed neutrality. To allow it, therefore, now to be passed over in silence, would be to recede from the full extent of our former pretensions, and give up at least half our rights. It is of no force to say that every country may do what it likes in spite of treaties, and that at the beginning of a new war neutrals might resist the principle, though they now admitted it. The difference in the two cases is great and striking. If the principle is now recognised by treaty at the commencement of a new war, should neutrals reject it, they would be the violators of the laws of nations. If it is now passed over in silence, and we should hereafter enforce it, they will be on the defensive, and we shall be endeavouring to establish a maritime code which, they will contend, cannot in justice be binding on them, since they never consented to its enactment. If, moreover, Buonaparte and his satellites think so lightly of the obligation of treaties, they ought to feel less repugnance at agreeing to our demands.'

'I hope you do not lay your account with coming to a gay metropolis. The town looks as dull as fogs and east winds can make it. Every other person one knows has measles or ophthalmia. The Chancellor is going to shut up the Opera. Scarcely one party is given in a week. Even at that nothing is to be seen but women yawning at each other. The only two things anybody says are, "Do you belong to the Argyle, and have you read 'Marmion'?" And before you have pronounced the first to be bad, and the second inferior to the "Lay," you are called upon to answer the same interrogatories to a dozen other people.'

In 1808 he visited Ireland, and gives a deplorable account of the roads about Killarney. He was enchanted with the beauty of the Lakes, but his pleasure was marred by the news of General Dalrymple's fiasco in Portugal; with characteristic bluntness he declared, 'If I were in the Cabinet I would have Dalrymple shot.'

In the autumn of the same year he made himself personally acquainted with the condition of his Sligo estates, and in the following letter we gain an interesting glimpse of the young peer as a landlord:

'Thursday I employed in walking and riding about the town of Sligo with Chambers, and Friday we took another ride over the whole of that part of the estate which lies connected by the sea-coast. I find there is a great deal, I may almost say, everything, to be done; and it will be absolutely necessary for me to repeat my visit next summer, and probably make it annual for some time. It is a tract of country about two miles broad and six long, bounded on one side by the sea, and on the other by bog and high, craggy mountains. It is wholly unimproved; but almost all the waste ground or bog is capable of being brought into cultivation, and all the arable may be rendered worth three times its present value. This, however, must be the work of time, and to accomplish it much must be done. The present objects which I must in the first instance set about are to put the parish church in a state of repair, so as to make it fit for service; to establish schools, to make roads, and to get rid of the middlemen in some cases where it can be accomplished. After that, as opportunities occur, I mean to endeavour to introduce a Scotch farmer to teach the people how to improve their land; to establish a little manufacturing village in a central part of the estate, where there are great advantages of water and stone; and to build a pier and make a little port near a village that stands on a point of land projecting into Donegal Bay, and called Mullaghmore.'

Lord Palmerston was not the man to shirk his responsibilities as a landowner, nor was he too much engrossed with politics or society to neglect the interests of the humble tenantry on his ancestral estates.

III

Secretary at War, 1809–1818

A MOST FLATTERING PROPOSAL WAS made to Palmerston in the year 1809. Perceval had become Prime Minister; and when at Broadlands Lord Palmerston received a letter from him 'desiring me to come to town immediately, as he had a proposal to make to me which he thought would be agreeable. I went up to him, and he offered me the Chancellorship of the Exchequer. I was a good deal surprised at so unexpected an offer, and begged a little time to think of it and consult my friends: Perceval said that if I declined to be Chancellor of the Exchequer, he should perhaps be able to offer to me the War Office.'

Young as he was for the high office thus placed at his disposal, he showed his sound sense by refusing to he dazzled by either the Chancellorship of the Exchequer or by a seat in the Cabinet. He chose the War Office *without* the latter distinction, and that decision shaped his whole career as a statesman. In a letter to his warm friend, Lord Malmesbury; dated October 16, 1809, he thus balances the pros and cons:

'Of course one's vanity and ambition would lead one to accept the brilliant offer first proposed; but it is throwing for a *great stake*, and where much is to be gained, *very much* also may be lost. I have always thought it unfortunate for anyone, and particularly a young man, to he put above his proper level, as he only rises to fall the lower. Now, I am quite without knowledge of finance, and never but once spoke in the House. The approaching session will he one of infinite difficulty. Perceval says that the state of the finances of this country, as calculated to carry on the war, is very embarrassing; and from what has lately happened in public affairs, from the number of speakers in opposition, and the few debaters on our side of the question, the warfare of the House of Commons will certainly be for us very severe. I don't know upon which of the two points I should feel most alarmed. By fagging and assistance I might get on in the office, but fear that I never should be able to act my part properly in the House.

'I should myself strongly incline to being Secretary at War. From what one has heard of the office, it seems one better suited to a beginner, and in which I might hope not to fail, or in which one would not be so prominent if one did not at first do as well as one ought to do.

'One consideration not to be wholly overlooked is, that we may probably not remain in long enough to retrieve any blunders made at the outset; and the ground of the War Office is, I think, *quite* high enough for me to leave off upon. Our party is certainly ill off for second-rates, but if Perceval cannot find another as good as me for the Exchequer, it's clear, I think, that we are too weak to stand.'

Malmesbury replied, urging him to accept the War Office *with* a seat in the Cabinet. To this Palmerston responded:

'Perceval having very handsomely given me the option of the Cabinet with the War Office (if I go to it), I thought it best on the whole to decline it; and I trust that, although you seemed to be of a different opinion at first, you will not, on the whole, think I was wrong. The office is one which does not invariably, or, indeed, usually go with the Cabinet. A seat there was consequently not an object to me for appearance' sake; and considering how young I am in office, people in general, so far from expecting to see me in the Cabinet by taking the War Office, would perhaps only wonder how I got there. With the Exchequer it would have been necessary, but with the War Office certainly not; and the business of the Department will, I take it, be quite sufficient to occupy one's time without attending Cabinet Councils. It would undoubtedly have been highly interesting; but for all purposes of business or debate, Perceval will of course keep one sufficiently informed to answer all one's wishes, at first at least.'

'Admiralty: *Oct.* 27, 1809.—It was yesterday settled that I should be Secretary at War, and I accordingly entered upon my functions this morning. There appears to be full employment in the office, but at the same time not of a nature to alarm one, and I think I shall like it very much.'

The duties of the post upon which this young man of twenty-five thus entered were very different from those which now fall upon the Secretary for War of to-day. There was then a Secretary for War, responsible for the policy and field operations, and a Commander-in-Chief who looked after discipline, recruiting, and promotions. It was the work of the office which Palmerston now held to control, or attempt to control, military expenditure, and to supervise and keep all the needful accounts. That he was fully alive to the opportunities for work to which the post invited him, his letters show:

'There is a good deal to be done; but if one is confined it is some satisfaction to have some real business to do: and if they leave us in long enough, I trust much may be accomplished in arranging the interior details of the Office. The business is to superintend all the accounts of the army, the militia, and volunteers; and from the great increase of our military establishments of late years, there is an immense arrear of accounts unsettled and daily accumulating. It will be a very fatiguing situation, and I fancy admits of scarce any holidays during the course of the year. However, one must do something, and if one can make oneself useful one must submit to a certain degree of inconvenience and labour.'

In 1809 great preparations were made at every place in town and country for illuminations, and distribution of food to help the poor to take part in celebrating the Jubilee of George III; and Lord Palmerston gave the most minute instructions as to what he wished to take place at Broadlands.

The unfortunate expedition to Walcheren is jokingly mentioned in the same correspondence: 'As to the further objects of the expedition, you must excuse me if I abstain from committing myself. The only information which I am at present at liberty to communicate is that Lord Chatham, and Sir Robert Strachan (the commanders of the British forces by sea and land) are to be instantly created Duke of Walcheren and Baron Rompert. Sir Eyre Coote is said to have the promise of a considerable grant of Verdonkenland. These arrangements are to he effected without delay lest any unforeseen event should render it desirable for us to evacuate the Scheldt. As to Sir Arthur Wellesley, it is amazingly provoking that he should have lost an opportunity of annihilating Victor. He came up with him at Talavera, attacked his outposts on the 22nd, and drove them in. He meant to make a general attack on the 23rd, but the Spanish general who had joined him made objections to that day, and prevailed on Wellesley to postpone it till the 24th. In the meantime Victor, who knew his own weakness, broke up and marched off towards Madrid. This was very odd, as Cuesta is good for nothing but fighting, of which he is particularly fond. He never won a battle in his life, and never will, but he always puts himself in the front of battle, although he gives few orders, and those very bad ones. However, Spanish affairs are now a very secondary consideration. It has been clearly proved that the Spaniards have neither the energy nor the means to defend themselves, and they will, therefore, follow the fate and fortune of Austria. They have not, in the course of the war, found one general capable of commanding a brigade. They have done nothing since the Austrian campaign began; and now, after a respite of four months, they have not one army capable of making any resistance. Desultory individual efforts they can and will make, but war upon a large scale is above them.'

He was now hard at work with his official duties, and the news from the war in the Peninsula was for the next few years the all-engrossing subject of his thoughts. Yet he was too sensible a man not to allow himself brief spells of recreation: 'I went down,' he writes in 1810, 'to Conyers on Monday and returned on Tuesday. The day was terribly stormy and blew an absolute hurricane, and therefore I killed only a brace of pheasants. Lamb (Lord Melbourne) was luckier, and always found the wind lower when he fired, by which means he killed four brace ... I enclose a draft for £50 for the Romsey people as usual. Tell William he may hunt Pitch whenever he likes, and I am sure he will be well and pleasantly carried.'

In the House of Commons, in the speech in which, for the first time, he moved the Army Estimates, he made the following statements, which are quite in his later *civis Romanus sum* style, and which show him in his true character, as an ardent upholder of the power and fighting ability of the nation. 'The masculine energies of the nation were never more conspicuous, and the country never at any period of its history in so proud and glorious a position. After a conflict for fifteen years against an enemy whose power has been progressively increasing, we are still able to maintain the war with augmenting force, and a population, by the pressure of external circumstances, consolidated into an impregnable military mass. Our physical strength has risen as the crisis that required it has become more important, and if we do not present the opposition of those numerous fortresses to invaders which are to be found on the Continent, we do present the more insuperable barrier of a high-spirited, patriotic, and enthusiastic people.' This was quite the tone which age did not impair, and which sprang from the healthy mind in a healthy body, making him in the eyes of the people the very ideal of English manliness and pluck.

Palmerston limited himself to his department, taking little part in general debates. A very characteristic passage of arms took place between him and the Commander-in-Chief; Sir David Dundas, who regarded the Secretary at War as a subordinate, named only to execute the orders he issued. Palmerston stubbornly refused to view his office in this light. He said he considered himself placed as a sort of barrier between the military authority of the officers in command of the army and the civil rights of the people, and no alteration in this situation can take place without the interference of Parliament.' Against both Dundas, and later on the Duke of York also, Palmerston insisted upon the clear recognition of the authority of his department, and his right of direct and personal access to the King on all matters of importance connected with it.

On May 11, 1812, Percival was assassinated in the lobby of the House of Commons, and in the new Government which Lord Liverpool formed Palmerston remained in the War Office. It was at this time that he took the line he always adhered to in the future with regard to giving the franchise to Catholics, and the following significant passage occurs in a speech which he made in 1813 on that subject.

'Is it wise to say to men of rank and property, who from old lineage or present possessions have a deep interest in the commonweal, that they live in a country where, by the blessings of a free constitution, it is possible for any man, themselves only excepted, by the honest exertion of talents and industry in the avocations of political life, to make himself honoured and respected by his countrymen, and to render good service to the State; that they alone can never be permitted to enter this career; that they may indeed usefully employ themselves in the humbler avocations of private life, but that public service they can never perform, public honour they shall never attain? What we have lost by the continuance of this system it is not for man to know; what we might have lost can be more readily imagined. If it had unfortunately happened that by the circumstances of birth and education a Nelson, a Wellington, a Burke, a Fox, a Pitt, had belonged to this class of the community, of what honours and of what glory might not the page of British history have been deprived? To what perils and calamities might not this country have been exposed? The question is not whether we would have so large a part of the population Catholic or not. There they are, and we must deal with them as we can. It is in vain to think that by any human pressure we can stop the spring which gushes from the earth. But it is for us to consider whether we will force it to spend its strength in secret and hidden courses, undermining our fences and corrupting our soil, or whether we shall at once turn the current into the open and spacious channel of honourable and constitutional ambition, converting it into the means of national prosperity and public wealth.'

In 1816 he encountered in debate the man who had written so disparagingly of him when a youth, about to fight his first political battle, namely, Lord Brougham. 'The hon. and learned member has made an accusation, which I certainly cannot retort upon that honourable gentleman himself, namely, that he very seldom troubles the House with his observations; and at all events will abstain from all declamation and from any dissertation on the Constitution, and confine myself to the business at present in hand, the Army Estimates of the current year.'

In the year 1818 an attempt was made by an insane man to assassinate him, but, fortunately, he escaped with a slight wound.

Palmerston continued steadily to labour for the increased efficiency of the army, and this period of his life made him form opinions as to the duty that English statesmen owed to England in making her worthy of the place of a great nation, by the maintenance of forces by land and sea, which he was able in higher offices to give effect to, and adequately enforce. His power of repartee made him dreaded in debate. In reply to the stern economist Mr Hume, he declared that he had 'heard of an ancient sage, who said that there were two things over which even the immortal gods had no power, namely, past events and arithmetic. The hon. gentleman, however, seemed to have power over both.'

After the overthrow of Napoleon at Waterloo, and the conclusion of peace, Lord Palmerston, in common with large numbers of his countrymen, enjoyed what had become only a memory to most Englishmen—a trip to Paris. His office had brought him into the closest contact with the operations that led to Bonaparte's defeat, and he naturally took a keen interest in the consequences of that defeat.

Occasionally he visited France, and always made notes of the events of the hour. In 1815 he attended a review at Paris, and says: 'The foreign troops all march with a shorter and more constrained step than ours. The Emperor of Russia was so much struck with the active swinging step of our men that he ordered his troops immediately to adopt it. In two days afterwards he had a body of them out in the Champ de Mars. The men, as might naturally be expected, were confused and puzzled between the step they were used to and that which they were now required to march with. The consequence was they marched remarkably ill. The Emperor was in a great passion, and put three colonels of regiments into close arrest in one of our guard-rooms. His aides-de-camp thought themselves lucky that he did not order them to dance like Vestris, at twenty-four hours' notice, under penalty of being sent to Siberia.' He gives also an account of a review of the Russian army:

'The troops manoeuvred with great quickness and accuracy, and the Duke of Wellington was much pleased with their manner of deploying from column. He said he was satisfied that our manner of advancing in line instead of in column was one reason why we had always beaten the French. That if troops are steady, and the line is well formed, the line will always have an advantage over the column, from presenting so much larger a front of fire; and that by attacking the column rapidly they are prevented from deploying, which is an operation that cannot be performed under a close fire. The object of the column attack is to penetrate into the enemy's position and deploy in their rear; if he suc-ceeds in this the result is certain. Twice in the Peninsula the French had established a column on our position at Busaco and Albuera, but in each instance they were immediately charged by fresh troops and destroyed. At Busaco the Duke had had a regiment of Portuguese militia to make a road; the work had, however, been done before they came, and he was going to send them back. They begged that as a battle was likely to take place they might be kept; he consented, and desired them to remain on the very ground where they then were. This happened in the course of the action to become an important point, and the French made a great effort to get possession of it. The militia soon found that they had made a hard bargain of it, and lost no time in debating who should go away first. The Duke, however, immediately brought up two British regiments, and before the French column could deploy on the ground it had seized, it was cut to pieces. He said he had not above 16,000 to 18,000 British infantry at Waterloo; that he started with the very worst army that ever was got together; but that four or five regiments who had been in the Peninsula soon gave a tone and character to the entire army. The other troops under his command did very well. The Nassaus ran away, and fired at him when he rode up to rally them.

The Prussian army started with double his force, but by the time he reached Paris he was as strong as they were, though he had received no reinforcements, and they had not lost any great number in battle. But their discipline was so relaxed that their numbers rapidly diminished during the march. He had brought 60,000 to Paris, and they not more. The system of individual plunder had been the ruin of the French army, and would be the destruction of the Prussian. When officers were allowed to make requisitions for their troops they soon made them for themselves, and those who demanded provisions to-day would make demands for money to-morrow. War then assumed a new character. The profession of arms became a mercenary speculation, and the officers' thoughts grew to be directed towards the acquisition of plunder instead of the attainment of glory. The Duke had succeeded in keeping his army well in hand. No officer was permitted to make any requisition himself, but was obliged to state his wants to the Commissary, who applied to the agents of the French Government for the articles required; and, the supply being made through channels known to the people, and by authorities recognised by them, the burthen was not felt to be so oppressive as if the exaction had been made by the immediate order of an enemy, and at the caprice of individual officers. The consequence was that, though both the Prussians and ourselves lived equally at the expense of the country, the first are detested and the latter liked. The inhabitants who deserted their villages at the approach of the Prussians returned the moment our troops came in, and, confidence being restored, provisions followed of course. The difficulty of raising contributions in money in France was very great, there being no large fortunes. Property was very much subdivided. The *noblesse*, of course, had been ruined, and those of the *nouveaux riches* who had made large fortunes had been compelled by Buonaparte to spend them in supplying and equipping his army. One was ordered to find forage, another shoes, a third trousers, so that he treated them like leeches, allowed to suck only to disgorge.

'Nothing, he thought, could surpass or indeed equal the British troops in the field. The sense of honour among officers existed in no other service to the same degree. He felt always confident when he put a detachment into a post that they would maintain it against any force till they dropped. We did not look so well in a review as some of the others, and, indeed, he thought we paid too little attention to the dress and smartness of our men; and that in a military point of view the *tenue* of a soldier was of importance, and that he would he more likely to be orderly and well-behaved if obliged to be attentive to the neatness of his appearance. He seemed to think the cuirasses good things, and that they might be adopted with advantage by our heavy cavalry.'

During his stay in Paris, Lord Palmerston dined with Lord Castlereagh, where, he says, were present Lord Kinnaird and an old *intrigante,* the Baroness de Vaudemont. She began to attack Lord Castlereagh about the restitution of the pictures taken by the French from various European nations, and these pictures were at the time being sent away from the Louvre. She said we were a set of *filibustiers*. 'But madam,' said he, in his quiet way, 'you French think that because we are very good to you we should also show all sorts of sentiment for you, but, although we have plenty of sentiment for the women, we have none at all for the men of your nation.'

'The Duke had his army out for a field day before Paris. He supposed his object to be to gain possession of some heights in front of Montmartre, or rather the brow of the hill itself. He detached part of two divisions from the right towards St. Denis to go round and take the supposed enemy in flank, while he himself attacked them in front.

He marched the army about a couple of miles across the country, describing a sort of quarter circle round Montmartre, and the manner in which the columns of infantry advanced, with occasional charges of cavalry and bayonet, gave one a perfect representation of the attack of an army in an engagement, with the exception that there was no firing. At last when those who did not understand his evolutions least expected it, he suddenly deployed the whole into two lines in the most beautiful order imaginable. There was then a general salute. The Sovereigns having taken part on the spot where they happened to be, the whole army marched by, in about an hour and a half. Nothing could exceed the precision and steadiness and rapidity with which the man were performed. There was no confusion at any point. The men got over the ground at a surprising pace; and, when the deployment was made at last, the lines were as correct as they could have been when on parade. The foreigners who had been in the Prussian review, where the whole thing had been diligently rehearsed for two days before-hand, and where the plain was covered with little posts with bunches of straw on the top of them, to point out to each division the ground it was to occupy, were surprised and astonished to find that no such preparations had been made on our part, and that Wellington set out to move an army of about 60,000 men with as much ease as he would have done to move a set of chessmen upon a board. It was some time before they could believe that no orders had been given or plan formed, and Prince Maurice Lichtenstein did not seem to credit it, till he had been assured of the fact by almost all our generals of division, whom he successively asked. They were also much struck at seeing the Blues and the Life Guards charge over two very deep and wide ditches, that ran on each side a road which they were ordered to cross, and which they effected with very little loss, having only three or four tumbles. That which our men did least well was marching by. The army was very much admired for its lightness and regularity and the care with which it was manoeuvred. The Highlanders and the horse artillery seemed particularly to excite attention, and though the proceedings at the gallery of the Louvre (the taking away of the pictures stolen from other countries) had put us out of favour with the Parisians, still there was a considerable number of French spectators, and many carriages full of ladies, a thing never seen at the Prussian reviews.'

'Dined at Verey's with, amongst others, Monsieur Bresson, a man who has been chief of the police under Buonaparte; He told us some anecdotes of the Buonaparte family. He said that Napoleon was very much swayed and influenced by them, and particularly by his sisters, who were clever and ambitious women, and who often made him change determinations which he had formed with apparent obstinacy. He said the brothers were, most of them, weak and foolish, and had all of them the inconceivable folly to imagine that, when they were sent to be sovereigns of conquered States, they were really meant to be independent kings, and that it was often difficult to convince them of their mistake. He was at Cassel when Jerome came to take possession of the Kingdom of Westphalia, and said that the little man strutted about and gave orders to the right and left just as if he were fixed there for eternity, and when Nervins hinted to him something about the Emperor, he replied with admirable dignity, "Sachez que je suis Empereur chez moi." Nervins, however, whose particular business it was to keep him in order, suggested that perhaps the Emperor might send a general of division to take possession of his kingdom if he gave himself too many airs; and Jerome appears at length to have been accessible to the force of such persuasive reasoning.

'One day at a levée a courier arrived with despatches from Buonaparte. Nervins, who had sent complaints of Jerome, and entreated Buonaparte to give him a lecture, was curious to see how it would be taken, and maliciously pressed the little King to let them know what the Emperor said. Jerome opened the letter, and with the utmost coolness and self-possession read it aloud to the ministers and persons present, and as he read it, it ran that Buonaparte was delighted to hear how well he went on; that his administration was so prudent and popular, his finances so flourishing and his army so well established, that he every day saw fresh reason to approve the choice he had made of him for that kingdom, and ended by assuring him of his undiminished affection and regard. Nervins smiled at the manoeuvre, and having observed that a tall officer of hussars had taken advantage of his superiority of stature to crane over little Jerome's shoulders while he was reading the letter, he asked him as they went out what he thought of the letter. "Think of it?" replied the officer, "I never was so thunderstruck in my life. Why, would you believe it? I read the letter over the King's shoulder, and it was word for word the direct contrary of what he read in so unhesitating a manner to us."'

Ever anxious to pick up knowledge useful to him as Secretary at War, Palmerston visited Paris again in 1818 for the purpose of seeing the last of the allied armies on French soil. At Cambray he met at dinner Alava, the Spanish general who had been our ally in the campaigns of the Peninsula. Alava in the evening told us in a sneering manner, strongly demonstrative of the feeling of contempt that Spaniards entertain for the Portuguese, "A foreign officer wants a *gros* Portuguese to march quicker: he means to say '*vivo*'—that is, 'go on;' but he says '*viva*,' which being a compliment, the *gros* Portuguese stops and takes off his hat, making a low bow."'

Lord Palmerston was present at the Grand Review, and gives a full account of it, from which we take a few extracts:

'We reached the ground by 10 o'clock, and found the army drawn up ready to receive the Sovereigns—their right to the left of the road from Cambray to Quesnoy, their left upon the old road to Valenciennes. They were in close columns—the Danes on the extreme left, the British next, then the Hanoverians, then the Saxons and the Prussians. The supposed object of the movement of the day was to take possession of the height of Famars, in order to reconnoitre thence the town of Valenciennes, that of Bouchain being supposed to be in the hands of the enemy. The army of the enemy was represented by some Cossacks, some artillery, and the staff corps of the cavalry, and some infantry. Their infantry was supposed to be posted behind the Escaillon, and their cavalry to occupy the open country between that river and the Selle, which latter was immediately in front of our position. The armies were thus separated by two rivers, and the space between those rivers was in the hands of the foe. The plan of the day's movements was drawn out by the Duke and, Sir G. Murray, and the Duke told me he could not help fancying he was writing a harlequin farce.

'We had ridden about half-way down the line, beginning with our troops on the left, when the advance of cavalry took place, preceded by a hurry-scurry of Cossacks. We were in the middle of it, and obliged to dodge to the right and left to avoid the different bodies which were riding away, as the lie of the ground rendered their descent to the river most easy. We crossed the Selle with the artillery, and saw some very pretty manoeuvring of the British cavalry. We then went away to the right to see the advance of the Prussians, who were to turn the flank of the enemy, and crossed the Escaillon with them near Bermerin. Their advance was regular, but slow. They had been practising the mar upon the very ground, so that it was all familiar to them. Lord Beresford, with whom we were riding, said, "Does not that opposite brow, with those solid columns scattered about, look like a gentleman's park and its plantations?" They seemed to have fewer officers than our troops. They certainly are slow movers, and it would not be easy to extricate them from any difficulties in which they might be entangled. Having continued with the Prussians until they and the Saxons got to Querenain, we rode across till we met the redcoats advancing in three lines to the front attack which was to finish the brief operations of the day. It was not national prejudice that made us exclaim at once "How beautiful!" The superiority of our troops in activity and facility of manoeuvre is now universally admitted.

'Half-way up the first height a charge of bayonet was ordered, and, with that "Hurrah" which can never be heard by an English heart without emotion, our troops rushed forward and in a few minutes crowned the height.

'After the last charge of cavalry, and before the marching past, the Duke took Alexander down to see a new pontoon bridge. The Duke availed himself of the occasion to say what he thought of him and his army, and praise from such a quarter would not fail to have its due effect. I had a great deal of conversation with the Duke. He observed that the Prussians were showing us the three kinds of columns used in modern war. The column of one battalion, the column of two or three used by the Prussians, and the great mass employed by the French, consisting of three lines one behind the other; and each line containing three battalions in column abreast of each other.

'"Look," said he, pointing to one of these masses, "how formidable that looks; and yet I defy the French" (clapping one hand against the other) "to mention any one instance in the whole war in which these masses had made the slightest impression on our lines." The way he usually met them was to cover his lines behind any little rising ground that might be at hand, and let the mass come on. Then, when they got within a fair distance, he used to order his men to stand up, to advance, and to open a fire upon the mass. The effect of the fire of a long line on five or six thousand men huddled up together like sheep in a fold, was necessarily destructive. On the other hand, none but the outside men could fire to any purpose. Still, however, it was usually found that they all began firing. "Then," said he, "these thick columns begin to waver; and as an instance of what an odd thing human nature is, it was invariably those in the rear, who were furthest away from danger, that were the first to run away. As the French columns ran from the rear, one used to see the men huddling together and running to the right or left, just as they saw the means of sheltering themselves behind a body of fellow fugitives, so that at a little distance they went waddling like ducks. At Waterloo a column of French were firing across the road at one of our regiments. Our people could not get at them to charge them because they would have been disordered by crossing the road. It was a nervous moment. One of the two forces must go about in a few minutes—it was impossible to say which it might be. I saw about two hundred men of the 74th who seemed to have had more than they liked of it. I formed them myself about twenty yards from the flank of the French column, and ordered them to fire, and in a few minutes the French column turned about." This anecdote, related simply and incidentally without the least parade, shows the dangers he exposed himself to in battle.'

In 1820, George IV, who never liked Lord Palmerston, succeeded to the Throne; Napoleon died in 1821; Castlereagh in the following year, when Canning became Foreign Minister, a post soon to be exchanged for that of Prime Minister. Lord Palmerston wrote in 1824 the following note in view of Russian advances on Turkey, and the proposed mediation of Great Britain:

'To preserve the peace of the world is the leading object of the policy of England. For this purpose it is necessary in the first place to prevent to the utmost of our power the breaking out of new quarrels; in the second place, to compose, where it can be done by friendly mediation, existing differences; and, thirdly, where that is hopeless, to narrow as much as possible their range. Fourthly, to maintain for ourselves an imperturbable neutrality in all cases where nothing occurs to affect injuriously our interests or our honour. With respect to the mediation itself; it is almost unnecessary to say that the extent to which we should be prepared to go is only that of an intervention strictly amicable; but that we are not disposed in any case to join either party in the war, and that we could not consent to hold out a menace which we have no design to carry into execution.'

These sentences show that early, as late, in his political career he set before himself the ideal that Britain's office was to be an active agent in promoting peace, and in maintaining for that end the balance of power among the European nations.

IV

In the Cabinet and in Opposition, 1827–1830

DURING THE YEARS 1824–1827 Palmerston had leisure enough to look after his Irish properties, and to undertake works for their benefit at Sligo. Some time was spent in trying to improve the Irish estates and the industrial habits of the people on them. He sought to reclaim sterile and marshy lands and to improve the condition of his tenants.

The following extracts from his correspondence show that he threw himself into his duties as a landlord with all his customary energy and shrewdness:

'*August* 5, 1825.—I am going in a fortnight to Sligo again, to see the progress of my harbour, and to settle some further improvements with Mr Nimmo, the civil engineer whom I have employed to survey my bogs. He recommends me to lay down an iron railroad of about six miles in length, by means of which I should be enabled to bring up a shelly sand from the sea-beach to reclaim the bogs, and to carry down in return to my new harbour turf from the bogs, prepared as fuel; and he thinks that a very considerable export trade of this turf could be carried on with the town of Sligo and the coast beyond it. This would require a capital of between five and six thousand pounds to be immediately laid out; but I am inclined to think it will answer, and I could get the money advanced by the commissioners in Ireland, who are authorised by Parliament to issue Exchequer bills in aid of public works of this kind for the internal improvement of Ireland, taking repayment by annual instalments of so much per cent. added to the interest. But this matter I shall settle when on the spot.'

The following letter is still more interesting because of its comments on public affairs:

'Londonderry: *Oct.* 21, 1826.—I went on to Sligo, where I remained eighteen days, the greater part of the time at Cliffony, with Nimmo the engineer, looking over the progress of my improvements, and planning arrangements for the future. My harbour is nearly completed, and will be an excellent one for my purposes: it will be about one and a quarter English acres in extent, and will have fourteen feet water at high spring tides—enough depth to admit vessels of 300 tons, and as much as any harbour on the west coast of Ireland, and it has an excellent anchorage in front of it, where ships may wait the tide to enter.

'I have been planting bent upon a great tract of blowing sand, and I think with success. I have about 600 acres of that description on the coast, and this year I planted bent on about 140 acres, which only cost me £50. The bent was taken up from parts where it grows in clusters, and planted closely in rows fourteen feet apart; it is almost all growing, and I see that in another year it will very much stop the sand, and I have no doubt that, by extending my plantation, I shall succeed in covering the greater part of the 600 acres with green bent, and when that has stopped the blowing of the sand it soon gives way to grass, but it is itself very good food for cattle. I have established an infant linen market at Cliffony, and have no doubt of its prospering. I have got two schools on foot, but am at war with my priest, who forbids the people to send the children. I know that if I was resident I should beat him in a moment, and I hope to do so even though an absentee. I am getting the people to build some houses according to a plan Nimmo and I have laid out, and as a proof that my tenants and I are not on bad terms, I found one fellow was building a good house, two stories high and to have a slated roof; which will cost £150, on a piece of ground of which he has no lease. I have established a limekiln. I have a great mind when I go to Cambridge to find some zealous Simeonite who would curb the ardent enthusiasm which would impel him to the Ganges, and might content himself with winning his Jerusalem spurs by a campaign in the parish of Ahamlish.

'The Catholic and anti-Catholic war is, however, carried on more vigorously than ever, and the whole people are by the ears, like an undisciplined pack of hounds. It is most marvellous, to be sure, that sensible statesmen should be frightened by the bugbear of foreign interference clashing with domestic allegiance, and should see with calmness and apathy a civil war raging throughout Ireland, engrossing all the thoughts and passions of the people, diverting them from the pursuits of industry, and retarding the progress of national prosperity, and menacing, in the event of foreign hostilities, inconveniences of the most formidable and embarrassing description. I can forgive old women like the Chancellor, spoonies like Liverpool, ignoramuses like Westmorland, old stumped-up Tories like Bathurst; but how such a man as Peel, liberal, enlightened, and fresh-minded, should find himself running in such a pack is hardly intelligible. I think he must in his heart regret those early pledges and youthful prejudices which have committed him to opinions so different from the comprehensive and statesmanlike views which he takes of public affairs. *But the day is fast approaching, as it seems to me, when this matter will be settled as it must be*; and in spite of the orgies in this town and Armagh, the eloquence of Sir George Hill and Lord G. Beresford, and the bumpers pledged to the "'Prentice Boys'" motto of "No surrender," the days of Protestant ascendancy I think are numbered. It is strange that in this enlightened age and enlightened country people should be still debating whether it is wise to convert four or five millions of men from enemies to friends, and whether it is *safe* to give peace to Ireland.'

Early in 1827 Lord Liverpool died. His party had ranged themselves under the leadership of Lord Eldon on the one hand, and of Canning on the other. The latter triumphed in the ensuing struggle. Canning succeeded to the premiership. Palmerston had previously thrown in his lot with Canning, and hence probably was not greatly surprised at the receipt of the following letter:

'Foreign Office: *April* 1827.—My dear Lord, I should be very glad of a few minutes' conversation with you, any time after 4 this afternoon. Very sincerely yours, GEO. CANNING.'

On the back of this note there is written the following in Lord Palmerston's hand:

'Canning informed me he wished me to be either Secretary of State for Home Department or Chancellor of the Exchequer, that the King made a point of having an anti-Catholic in the first office, but if he could not be found, which was probable, Canning would like me to be there. If not, he should wish me to be Chancellor of the Exchequer. Sturges Bourne was afterwards made Home Secretary, and it was settled that I should be Chancellor of the Exchequer, and Canning wished me to take the office immediately, so as to have my writ moved the first day after the recess. I wished to delay it until the end of the session, because, as Sir John Copley had just been made Chancellor (Lord Lyndhurst) and vacated his seat, and as Bankes and Goulburn and Tindal were going to fight for his seat, I felt that if I vacated then I should come into their contest, and at least be sure of much trouble if not worse results, as all three were anti-Catholic, and I alone for the Question. Canning on these grounds consented to let the matter stand over till the end of the session, but called me immediately to the Cabinet. In the meantime the Whigs joined the Government. Sir William Knighton felt that it would be a great convenience to him as Keeper of the Privy Purse, and to the King, to have Canning continue First Lord of the Treasury and Chancellor of the Exchequer, instead of being, as he wished, First Lord of the Treasury and Secretary of State for Foreign Affairs, making me Chancellor of the Exchequer. Herries, the Secretary to the Treasury, was an old friend of Knighton's. He was also a friend of Rothschild. Canning was from these quarters, I believe, though I don't actually know it, persuaded of that which, however, was really true, namely, that he ought, as Prime Minister, to be at the head of the Finance, and continue Lord of the Treasury and Chancellor of the Exchequer. He therefore, towards the end of the session, told me this change of arrangement in a manner very kind, but which showed that he felt he was doing an ungracious thing, stating that, at any future time when my situation as Secretary for War should be divested of the importance that then belonged to it by the reappointment of a Commander-in-Chief; I should, if I liked it, be made a Peer, and have any other practicable arrangement which might be agreeable to me; in short, gave me all these general assurances, which mean nothing at all. The fact was, as I believe, that Knighton and others thought that while Canning was Chancellor of the Exchequer, being also leader of the House of Commons and head of the Government, Herries, as Secretary of the Treasury, would of necessity be virtually Chancellor of the Exchequer, in consequence of the multiplicity of Canning's other occupations, but that if I were appointed, having nothing else to do, I should be effective in the office, and Herries would sink into a mere instrument. My reason for believing this is the great struggle which the King, urged on as I know by Knighton, made in August following, on Canning's death, to have Herries appointed Chancellor of the Exchequer instead of me, Goderich having again proposed me to the King for that office. Canning, at the interview last alluded to, told me that the King had said to him that he had good reason to know that the thing of all others which I should like would be to succeed the Duke of Manchester as Governor of Jamaica; that he, Canning, said he thought it very unlikely, but if the King really thought such a thing would be agreeable to me, the best way to ascertain the fact would be for him (Canning) to ask me the question. I could not help laughing so much at this idea that I perceived that I had unintentionally disconcerted Canning for an instant. He afterwards proposed to me to be Governor-General of India in succession to Lord Amherst. I told him how much I felt flattered at the offer of so distinguished an appointment, which was so legitimate an object of any man's ambition, but that the same offer had been made to me twice before, once in the summer of 1826 by Peel at Lord Liverpool's suggestion, and afterwards in November last by Courtenay, Secretary to the Board of Control, at Wynn's desire, but that I had on both those occasions declined an appointment which, from climate and distance, had to me objections which outweighed the very splendid inducements which it held out, and that my decision on those former occasions was founded upon full consideration of the matter, and the same motives led me now to decline. The fact is that I have the ill-luck, from many and various circumstances, to be displeasing to the King, and he would not willingly see me in any office which brought me in contact with him, and would be glad to get me civilly out of the way. He said to Madame de Lieven in August 1827, *"Connaissez-vous Palmerston?"* *"Oui, je l'ai connu bien depuis longtemps, mais ce n'est que dernièrement que je l'ai connu bien, et je vous assure que je l'aime beaucoup.*" "*Eh bien,* "said he, "*il y a quelque chose en lui qui me dépalaît, il a l'air toujours si fier.*" She answered him I was a "*bon garçon*"—an "*excellent garçon,*'" &c.

In this connection we may quote the following contemporary testimony as to Palmerston's manners at the time when he, like a later Prime Minister, had the reputation of being something of a dandy:

'I remember my mother used to tell us of her first recollections of Lord Palmerston, when she was a girl of fourteen or fifteen. Her father was at the Admiralty, and Lord Palmerston lived there also when he first started in official life. Her father was at that time always praising up this model young man as a pattern of industry and virtue, and prophesying that he would rise to the top of a tree. But she and her sisters used to think him very pedantic and very pompous, and laugh at him accordingly, and among them he went by the nickname of "Sir Charles Grandison," because he was so priggish and so sedate! She used to laugh about it, and say how strangely unlike his after character this was, but it must have been part of his determination to succeed.'

Although Canning only lived four months after becoming Prime Minister, far-reaching changes were introduced into the relations of political parties, and movements began which were to culminate in the great Reform Bill of 1832. The old Court party—the so-called 'Protestant,' and certainly the most reactionary, clique—began to disappear, and the modern Liberal party to emerge. Deserted by the Tories, Canning looked to the Whigs. What happened can best be given in Palmerston's own summary:

'Stanhope Street: *May* 4, 1827.—My dear William, all arrangements are now settled, at least as to general principle. The Whigs join us in a body and with zeal, and some of them will come into office immediately. I am in the Cabinet, but continue Secretary at War till the end of the session, having in addition to my own duties those of the Commander-in-Chief to perform. This is the natural constitution of my office, that in the absence of a Commander-in-Chief the patronage of the army devolves on the Secretary at War. At the end of the session I shall be Chancellor of the Exchequer, and then, in my opinion, some military man ought to be placed in the command of the army.

The advantage of the present arrangement is that it leaves the door open for the Duke of Wellington's return when the other arrangements are made, without dispossessing any individual. You will see by the debates that the Whigs have joined us manfully and in earnest, and have boldly faced all charges of inconsistency, declaring that they know it to be impossible that the Catholic question should be made a Cabinet measure, and do not join us upon any such expectation, but simply because they see as well as Peel that the having Canning at the head of the Government must of itself necessarily give a great advantage to the question; and because they agree with him on almost all other great questions of foreign and domestic policy; and because, if they did not support him, he could not, by reason of the defection of his colleagues, maintain his position. Nothing can be more satisfactory to Canning than the footing on which their accession is placed; he gives up no opinion either on parliamentary reform or any other question, and distinctly said so last night in the House. They make him a compliment of most of the questions on which they differ with him. He, in the first place, makes his Government and carries it through the session, and they come in as joining a Government already formed, and not as original ingredients in its composition.'

During the years in which Canning and the Duke of Wellington were the chief political personages, Peel's star was rising. Palmerston's place remained the same, Secretary at War. Canning died in August, 1827, his Ministry thus lasting only four months; but it marks the starting-point of English political progress and reform in the nineteenth century. Troublous times followed. Canning was succeeded by Lord Goderich, whose Ministry lasted only eight days longer than Canning's, and on January 25, 1828, the Duke of Wellington became Prime Minister. Lord Palmerston was soon summoned to an interview by the Duke, and has left the following record of what passed on the question of his joining the Cabinet:

'Before I gave the Duke of Wellington my final answer, I wished to have some distinct explanation upon one or two points. First, I concluded that his Government is to be upon the same understanding as Liverpool's and Canning's as to the Catholic question, *viz.* that every member of the Cabinet is to be at liberty to propound the question either in the Cabinet or in Parliament according to his own discretion. To this he entirely assented. I then said that I should wish an assurance that the patronage of the Government should be administered and its influence exerted, upon all occasions and by all its members, in a spirit of strict neutrality with reference to the Catholic question; and particularly that the support to be given to candidates at elections should not depend upon the opinions which such candidates may hold upon that question; and I wished, thirdly, that it should be understood that the Lord-Lieutenant and Chief Secretary in Ireland should at no time be persons decidedly hostile to the Catholic claim—a condition which I said was, I thought, essential to tranquillity in that country. He seemed to feel like a person who was more used to impose than to receive stipulations, and was disinclined to come to any specific assurance, laughing the matter off by saying that the first was asking him whether he was an honest man, and the second whether he was a madman—that he had himself governed Ireland, and knew that to send such a person as I described would be to blow up a flame in the country, and that he had no intention of doing any such thing. I said with respect to the first, that I had no distrust of him or of Peel; but that, when I saw Bathurst in high office, and Goulburn at the Treasury, and when I looked hack to what I knew had been done in former times, I could not consider such an understanding as unnecessary. He said; "Well, then, I may send in your name." I said that I considered these matters of more importance than he seemed to do, and that I must take time to think the matter over, and we parted, saying that he should hear from me again ... I have no doubt that the Duke will give me such an assurance as ought to be satisfactory between man and man.'

The Canningites—Huskisson, Lamb, Dudley, Palmerston, and others—acted with the Duke, but without any cordiality, and his administration was doomed from the start. It lasted only three hundred and one days. Palmerston sums up in a sentence the part played by his section: 'We joined the new Government in January. We left it in May. We joined as a party; as a party we retired.' They sided with Huskisson in the great quarrel which he had with Wellington, and in June, 1828,

Palmerston for the first time was in opposition. His correspondence gives us glimpses of the state of affairs at this time.

In a letter to his brother, dated Stanhope Street, June 8, 1828, he writes:

'I will send you the "Mirror of Parliament," which will contain a pretty accurate report of the debate of last Monday about Ministerial explanations. Peel declares that no change of measures or of policy will take place, and perhaps it may be so. I do not think that any material change can take place as long as he remains in the Government, because he is perfectly liberal and enlightened on all subjects except the Catholic question, on which indeed I suspect that he is quite of your opinion but is bound by early pledges. It is not at all impossible, too, that the other members of the Government may be more disposed to be liberal, now that they will themselves have the credit of whatever they may do in that line, than they were when they might be supposed to be swayed by their colleagues. This is not unnatural, and, from what I have lately heard, seems to be the case. At all events, if they do not pursue a liberal course, the Government cannot possibly stand. The opinion of Parliament and the country is decidedly that way, and if they were to try to run counter to it they would be beat in the House of Commons and not supported by the country if they were then to dissolve. A dissolution, too, under present circumstances with an anti-Catholic Government would be too serious a thing in Ireland to be lightly encountered, and I do not think there will be one this year. It would look too like an attempt to get rid of the Finance Committee. The ejected Liberals are, for a nascent party, strong in Parliament. The new Government is somewhat too military to be very pleasing to the country, but it will go on until something happens untoward to discompose it. It is so many years since I have been entirely my own master that I feel it quite comical to have no tie, and to be able to dispose of my day as I like. I have ceased for a week to attend the War Office, though Hardinge has not yet begun. My speech on Monday has been generally approved of. Huskisson thanked me very warmly. His friends were delighted, while, on the other hand, none of the Tories could find fault with anything I said, but have rather taken the tone of crying up my speech as contrasting it with Huskisson's. The greatest praise I have had, however, has been some violent abuse from the Duke of Cumberland, who declares I am grown quite a Democrat. The other day Prince George said to the Duke of Clarence, "They say you are in favour of the Catholics I hope that is not true." "Yes, my little fellow," said Clarence, "I am, and as far as I know myself I always shall be, and so you may tell your father." I was much struck and amused with the contrast between these Dukes on two occasions. At the child's ball at St James's, which was given before Retford came in, Clarence was civil to me as usual, but nothing particular. Cumberland was very gracious, asked me much about you, begged to be remembered to you, said you were a very good fellow, and they were very sorry to lose you, and in short was as civil as possible. At the full-grown ball, the Monday after the change had taken place, Cumberland barely recognised me, and passed with a slight acknowledgment, and a simple "It's very hot to-night." Clarence, on the contrary, reached out his hand to me across three people, shook me with the greatest cordiality, and said, "I am very glad to see you," with great emphasis.

'Miguel in Portugal seems to be fast approaching the fate he deserves. They say Heytesbury is to be sent immediately to the head-quarters, Stratford Canning to Corfu. The policy of the Austrian Government in declaring for absolute independence for Greece is curious. I am, however, for taking her at her word. I am sure it would be the best arrangement.

'Though we have all parted, yet we have parted perfectly good friends, especially Peel and I.'

'Stanhope Street: *June* 27, 1828.—We are going on here quietly. Everybody and all parties seem determined to wait and watch, and see the result, and whether the declarations that have been made will he kept to. In the meantime there is no opposition, and it is well for the Government that there is not, for Peel is the only man in the House of Commons on the Treasury Bench who can make a speech as a minister should do. In the only two debates we have had, one about the shipping question, and the other about the £250,000 sent from French indemnities to Naslie's Palace, if it had not been for the assistance lent by Huskisson and Grant, the Government would not have made a very brilliant figure. Calcraft is a good, useful, and ready debater, but a man who changes sides so suddenly and singly fights at a great disadvantage; and his sharp style of debating will not do in his present position so well as when he fought on his own account only. Fitzgerald is unpopular in the House of Commons, although a clever man and able speaker—does not hit the House, as Burke said, between wind and water. Murray makes an elegant speech upon preparation, and with practice would be a useful debater, but it is too late in life for him to take up this exercise with hopes of excelling in it. However, the ship will sail well enough …

'The King is remarkably well in health, and stronger on his legs, and walked the other day all over Windsor Castle with a party from Ascot. The Duke of Cumberland says he loves us so much he means to settle here and send for his Duchess. The Duke of Sussex was talking of him to me the other day; I said how abominable it was for that man to come over here to do so much mischief; treating him as if he were a Ghibelline instead of a Guelph. He and Eldon and the rest must, however, be little satisfied with the result of their intrigue, for, though they have satisfied personal feelings, they have been utterly disappointed in heir political expectations; and are even worse off in politics than they were. The tone of public opinion has fairly overpowered them, and, at the moment when they thought everything within their reach, has wrested everything from their grasp. The declaration of the Duke in the Lords as to the Catholic question, let him mean what he may—and there are great differences of opinion as to what he does mean—has advanced that question immensely, because it throws overboard all objections on *principle*, and places the matter simply on the ground of comparative arrangement. As long as the Prime Minister declared that on no terms and no conditions would he ever consent to admit Catholics into Parliament, so long the anti-Catholics throughout the country had a clear course and knew what to do and what language to hold. But the moment the Minister says there is no invincible objection to their admission, and that he can imagine arrangements which would render such a measure harmless, the column is broken and every man looks to himself and his own feelings and opinions, and, finding his general meditates a retreat, determines not to be the last to stay. I expect, therefore, that our majority in the Commons next year will be very considerably increased. This cannot be very palatable to the Duke of Cumberland and Co. The exclusion of Eldon, the taking in of Calcraft, the overtures made to Lord Grey—all these things must be exceedingly distasteful to those persons who objected to the ejected as being too anti-Tory. Our session is now drawing nearly to a close.

'We may now hope to be in a settled state (as to finance) as the Government have positively determined to adhere to the abolition of the one-pound notes as fixed by the present law, which forbids any such note being issued after April, 1829, and this paper currency was the great element of all our convulsions and revulsions. While such notes pass current, gold cannot remain in the country; and when there is no gold, or at least only a small quantity, the law may require that notes should be convertible. But what is there to convert them into? And as to the bankers giving security, exchequer bills and estates and three per cents. cannot be coined into sovereigns when panic happens, and therefore do not guard against the evil. Panic will always be liable to happen as long as we have paper money, because there is a tendency in paper to become, every now and then, excessive, and, when the issuers think they have too much in circulation and begin to withdraw it, prices fail. The moment prices fall, there are more sellers than buyers, because all expect a greater fall, and the sellers hasten to get what they can, and the buyers wait for the lower price. Then comes bankruptcy by persons selling for less than they bought at, instead of for more. Then alarm, then run on banks, and if the banks have one-pound notes in the hands of poor people, who cannot afford to trust and wait, and if there is not a gold circulation to change the notes, stoppages follow, and extensive ruin and misery. Upon this point Government mean to stand or fall—and the public is with them.

'About Portugal—I cannot think that Miguel will stand. His proceedings are much too violent. He has certainly shut up upwards of two thousand people in Lisbon. No country can stand this sort of thing. There must be a reaction even among his friends, and when Palmella and Saldanha get to Oporto in their steamboat, which they probably will in spite of the blockade, the Pedroists will have the head they want. I fear, however, they want heart as much as head.'

In his journal Palmerston notes the significance of O'Connell's return for Clare, and the change of front going on in the Cabinet with regard to Catholic Emancipation:

'Irish affairs have gone on from bad to worse ever since the summer. *The Clare election began a new era, and was an epoch in the history of Ireland.* O'Connell did not at first mean to stand himself, but no eligible Protestant candidate could be found; and as all the landholders, with scarcely an exception, were for Fitzgerald, nothing perhaps but the influence of O'Connell as a candidate could have carried the point. The event was dramatic and somewhat sublime. The Prime Minister of England tells the Catholics, in his speech in the House of Lords, that if they will only be perfectly quiet for a few years, cease to urge their claims, and let people forget the question entirely, then, after a few years perhaps *something may be done for them.* They reply to this advice, within a few weeks after it is given, by raising the population of a whole province like one man, keeping them within the strictest obedience to the law, and, by strictly legal and constitutional means, hurling from his seat in the representation one of the Cabinet Ministers of the King. There were thirty thousand Irish peasants in and about Ennis in sultry July, and not a drunken man among them, or only *one*, and he an Englishman and a Protestant, and O'Connell's own coachman, whom O'Connell had committed upon his own deposition for a breach of the peace. No Irishman ever stirs a mile from his house without a stick; not a stick was to be seen at the election.

'Lord Anglesey *begged that when I got back to London, if I was able by any means whatever to pick up what were the intentions of the Government, I would write him word.* The Lord-Lieutenant of Ireland begging a private gentleman to let him know, if he could find out, what the Prime Minister meant upon a question deeply affecting the peace and welfare of the country which that Lord-Lieutenant was appointed to govern, and upon which question he was every week stating to the Government the opinions he himself entertained—a strange instance of the withholding of that confidence which, for both their sakes, ought to have existed. He said he had had a good deal of communication with the Catholics, and could answer for keeping them quiet for the present. They were contented with impartiality and justice. The Protestants, on the contrary, required partiality to themselves, and injustice to the Catholics. Still, some of those leading Protestants would be very glad to have the question settled for them by an overruling authority; as long as it remained unsettled they are compelled—or, rather think themselves compelled—to keep their places in their party by heading meetings,' &c.

Lord Palmerston's interest in foreign affairs continued to deepen, and early in 1829 he visited Paris again. He writes of French and Eastern affairs as follows:

'*July*, 1829.—Polignac expects to be taken into the (French) Government, and says that he is not afraid of the responsibility, and that the only way is to be strict and determined, and to *terrasser* one's opponents. If he acts upon this system he will *terrasser* himself in a short time. That system will not do in France unless he could abolish the Constitution, and it is now happily too late for such a man as Polignac to think of accomplishing a change like that. Madame d'Escars is come over probably with the hope of welding Polignac and his party with our King, but she has failed as yet in getting more than an hour's audience in London, instead of being invited down to the lodge at Windsor. She says, "*Que le bon Dieu me le pardonne, mais, pour vous avouer la vérité, j'adore le Duc de Wellington.*" This got round to the King, and, as he by no means partakes in that worship, did not much please him.'

On the Russian campaign in progress against Turkey he says in a letter to his brother William:

'The advantage gained by Diebitch over the Vizier was even more considerable than was at first supposed. The sooner the Turks get well thrashed in a pitched battle, the sooner they will agree to reasonable terms of peace, and it is only by making peace quickly that they can save their Danube fortresses, and, if those are once taken, it may not be so easy for them to get them back again, and it is quite certain that England never will spend a single shilling for this purpose. The Duke of Cumberland stays here, and has sent for his Duchess and son. This will annoy the Duke of Wellington, because the Duke of Cumberland is determined to get him out if he can, and, by being on the spot and with the King constantly, he has it in his power to blow into a flame every little difference between the King and the Government. The Monday before Parliament was prorogued, Cumberland went over to the King and advised him to object to any paragraph in the proposed speech which might convey an opinion that the settlement of the Catholic question had been a good thing, and accordingly when the Council met that day and the Duke showed the King the draft of the speech, the King struck out a whole paragraph about the Catholic question, and obliged the Duke of Wellington to go back and frame a new paragraph such as you saw, only expressing a hope, and no opinion. The King and Cumberland consider this as a victory over the Government, and as giving the King the upper hand with them, and proving that if he only resists them they will give way. They will not, however, do so upon all things. In the meantime matters at home are in a state in which they can hardly remain.'

The following letter from Palmerston to his brother-in-law gives a very clear view of the state of affairs immediately preceding the formation of Earl Grey's Administration:

'Shugborough: *October* 7, 1829.—My dear Sulivan, I arrived here the day before yesterday, Littleton having transferred his party to this place, on account of some private theatricals holding here in which Lord Anson and Lord and Lady Belfast performed with tolerable success, and divers other ladies and gentlemen with remarkable want of skill. I go to-day to Lord Anglesey's, and thence to Liverpool, where I shall take steam to Dublin. So at last peace is made between Russia and Turkey, and upon Russia's own terms. I hope and trust that Greece will now be placed upon a proper footing, and our Government will find that they have failed of both their objects, having succeeded neither in preventing the establishment of Greece, nor in protecting the Sultan from the arms of Russia. We shall, therefore, have lost our influence both with the free and the despot. This is the fate of those who are unable to pursue a straight course, because, their inclination leading one way and necessity driving the other, they are forced into the diagonal.

'I had a curious conversation on Saturday evening at the Travellers' with Sir Richard Vivian, the member for Cornwall. Sir William Heathcote had called on me at Broadlands last week, and told me he expected Vivian at Hursley, and that he would be sorry to find me absent from Hampshire. Finding Vivian at dinner at the club, I sat down by him and fell to forthwith to politics and cutlets, and the dialogue, ended in his proposing to me to be leader of the House of Commons to a Mansfield, Eldon, Newcastle, and Knatchbull Administration. I began by observing that the Duke seemed to be getting the Tories round again, and recovering his strength so as to be able to meet Parliament again without any reinforcements. Vivian said this was quite a mistake, that the Tories were more adverse than ever, that few people knew better than he did what they were about, that the Duke of Wellington was tottering more than ever, and that even in a fortnight or three weeks a new Government might be formed ; that the King had not seen his first Minister since some day in August, and was only watching for an opportunity to get rid of him; that, at all events, Peel could not possibly meet the House again as leader.

'He then asked how I felt myself and to what degree bound to Huskisson, whether I could and would take office without him, and whether I should he disposed to join such a Government as that he mentioned; that Huskisson frightened the country gentlemen; that I had only pledged myself on foreign politics, and was free about trade and currency; that I should probably feel no difficulty about leading the House of Commons. I said that, as to Huskisson and myself, we found ourselves from various circumstances acting together, and that we agreed in opinions, but that we were each of us free with respect to the other; that I should have no cause to complain if he accepted office without me, and I considered myself as having a similar freedom with respect to him; that, as to my opinions on trade and currency, it had certainly so happened that no occasion and opportunity had arisen for me to express them in Parliament in any detail, but that they were formed, and formed upon some reflection, and, as far as I could judge, were not likely to be altered, and that they were entirely in unison with that system which, though much older than Huskisson, was perhaps first carried extensively into practice by him, and which had exposed him to such undeserved censure; that consequently I should not be disposed to join any Government who intended to retrace the steps which Parliament has taken on these subjects ; that, as to joining any particular Government, all I could say was that I had no personal antipathies, but that no man could answer such a question in the abstract and by anticipation, but must first know who the men were who were to be proposed to him as colleagues, and what system of government they intended to pursue.

'He went on in the same way, and at length said that the question he had for some time been desirous of putting to me was whether I should have any objection to have my name mentioned to the King as willing to be Secretary of State for the Colonies, and leader of the House to such a Government as he had alluded to, saying that I should be a great card to them, and that the King might be more likely to agree to the formation of such a Government if he found that a certain number of persons were already willing to become members of it. He had in the commencement of the conversation expressed his opinion that the Duke of Wellington was a man of most unmeasured ambition, who wants to make all Europe a military camp and to govern upon arbitrary principles, in proof of which he adduced the recent establishment of Polignac in France and the late Police Bill here. My reply to this specific position was of course a negative. I said I certainly could not wish my name so to be mentioned to the King; that if any proposition was made to me by a Government already formed or in the act of being formed, my answer would be the same as that which I made to the Duke in 1828—"First tell me who are your men, and what are to be your measures and then I shall be able to say whether it would suit me to become your colleague."

'He then went on to discuss lightly various men, apparently with the view of letting me see indirectly how it was intended that the projected Government should be formed. Lord Mansfield would, he said, of course be the head. Eldon would be a member. Brougham, he thought, must be got out of the House of Commons, as he would be too formidable an antagonist, and why should he not make an excellent Chancellor? Lyndhurst had been tried and must go. Fitzgerald, he said, is a quick, clever fellow and would be most useful—did I think he would unite himself with such a Government? I said I thought he scarcely could or would join a Government formed upon the ruins of that of the Duke and Peel. Young Stanley he praised as a man that should be obtained, and he discussed whether Stanley would require a Cabinet office or would take one out of the Cabinet. Herries he commended as a man full of the most useful knowledge. Huskisson he mentioned in connection with the Chancellorship of the Exchequer. Robert Grant would make an admirable Speaker, and Charles Grant (who, I suppose, is too much identified with Free Trade for this party) might be made Governor of Jamaica. (This appointment, by the way, seems to be the Chiltern Hundreds of political men who are to be got out of the way.) Lord Grey was deemed impracticable as a colleague. Falmouth unmanageably obstinate. The Duke of Newcastle lauded generally for his good sense and understanding, and Sir E. Knatchbull pointed out as Secretary to the Home Department.

'My part in all this was chiefly that of listener and suggester of general remarks for the purpose of leading on the conversation. I said I should much doubt the success of such a Government as he was sketching out, and thought that no Government would sufficiently carry public opinion with it that did not contain more persons with whom as public men the country was already acquainted; that the King, too, must have some ostensible reason for changing his Government, and could not here do as in France, and send word one fine morning to his Ministers that he had appointed another lot; and that, moreover, the Government must be turned out for doing something or for not doing something, and that their successors must be bound to do the reverse of that, whether omission or commission, for which they were dismissed. This he treated very lightly, saying the King never could be at any greater loss for a reason to turn out his present Ministers than Russia always is for a reason to make war on Turkey; at all events, he said that if nothing were done before Parliament met, yet that the very first day, if the Tories and Whigs and Canningites would only unite in an Amendment, the Government must be beat. When we parted he asked where he should direct to me. He also remarked that the Duke of Cumberland was getting round again in public opinion.

'All this is curious as showing how busily Cumberland and Eldon are still at work and how much they flatter themselves with success in getting the Duke out, provided they can only hold out to the King the prospect of a decent Government. It is plain they have opened their eyes to the impossibility of making a purely Tory Government, and that they are now come to the next step, that is, to try to mix, with a predominance of old fellows saturated with the brine of Toryism, a few young men of the Liberal parties who shall not be able to set up as objectors to any course proposed. They wish to tempt me by brilliant offers to forego opinions to which I do not happen to be personally tied by any public declaration. I suspect that

Foreign Affairs are intended for Vivian himself. He is violently against the Metternich and Apostolical school of which the Duke and Aberdeen are disciples. Stanley they think would be a good decoy for the Whigs. As far as I individually am concerned, it seems to me that my interest as well as inclination leads me to adhere to the party with whom I am thrown. I consider myself as being free if I choose, because we never have met or consulted as a party, and have upon no occasion voted as a body. We sit together, but upon almost every question last session voted different ways. But as to going to the Tory party, even if they really and in good earnest were to propose to me to be their House of Commons leader, though I should not be quite in the same false position as Peel, because he has always concealed his opinions more or less, and I have avowed mine, yet still to belong to people you do not think with cannot answer. In fact, the only Government which could answer the wants of the nation would be one composed of men known and looked up to. The Duke has a great hold upon public feeling. No other individual now living has perhaps so great a one. Whether this is ill or well founded is nothing to the purpose, but so it is.'

Lord Palmerston had been now for some time out of office, and although he was invited by the Duke of Wellington to rejoin his Administration, the negotiation failed, as Lord Palmerston said he must vote in Parliament for a reform in the franchise.

We close this period of Lord Palmerston's life, his long apprenticeship to the public service, as it may be termed, with a letter written some years later, which throws a strong light upon the tangled politics of that day:

'Broadlands: *December* 21, 1838.—When Lord Goderich was turned out, and the Duke of Wellington sent for, in consequence of Goderich going to George IV and telling him that there was an irreconcilable difference between Huskisson and Herries, and that he, Goderich, did not know what to do, the Duke of Wellington sent for Huskisson, and asked him and the rest of Canning's friends to join the Government about to be formed. Huskisson then called a meeting of Canning's friends then in London, and C. Grant, Binning, Dudley, Littleton, and myself met at his house. Melbourne (then William Lamb) was at that time in Dublin, and I forget whether Warrender was at the meeting or not. The two questions which at that moment excited the deepest interest were the Catholic question and the recently concluded Greek treaty. The Tory party had stoutly opposed Catholic emancipation, and had utterly condemned the withdrawal of Greece from Turkish domination. Canning's party had been strongly for emancipation and for the Greek treaty. Huskisson told us that the inducement held out by the Duke to persuade us to join him was that, if we did so, the Government would be neutral as to the Catholic question, leaving that question an open one as it had hitherto been, and that if we declined he should be obliged to fill up his Government with men of the old Tory party, and the whole influence of the Administration would then be forthwith against emancipation. He said, moreover, that, if we joined him, the Greek treaty should be scrupulously acted upon, and that, as a security that Canning's system of foreign policy should be continued, the Foreign Office should be given to Lord Dudley, and that, as a security for a liberal commercial system, Charles Grant should have the Board of Trade. Having well considered all these matters, we determined that it became us to accept the Duke's offer, and we joined his Government. But we soon found that putting men of different opinions together does not unite them, and every day showed more and more the divergence of sentiments which prevailed. Then came the question about East Retford and Penryn, which led to the resignation of Huskisson and the rest of Canning's friends. In the September following happened the tragical death of Huskisson on the Liverpool and Manchester Railway.

'Soon after that event I received at this place a letter from the late Lord Powis, an old and intimate college friend, who wrote from Powis Castle asking me to meet him in London. I went, and he told me he had been requested by the Duke of Wellington to see me and to ascertain whether I would then join his Government. He wished to know who the persons were with whom I considered myself acting in public life, and said that, if I accepted, the Duke would make room for (I think) two of my friends in the Cabinet. I said at, once that Dudley, C. Grant, and W. Lamb were the persons with whom mainly I considered myself acting—that, no doubt, the offer was very handsome and flattering, but that I should not like to belong to the Government unless Lord Grey and Lord Lansdowne also were to become members of it, because I felt that I and my two friends would not alone and unsupported be enabled to make our views prevail when they might differ from those of other members of the Cabinet. I afterwards—the next day, I believe—was sent for by the Duke, and had a private interview with him at Apsley House, when he repeated what Lord Powis had been desired by him to say to me, and I repeated what I had said. Of course the condition which I attached to the acceptance of the Duke's offer put an end to the negotiation, because, as he said, though he might have the means of creating two or three vacancies, he was not prepared for such a remodelling of the Administration as the admission of Lord Grey and Lord Lansdowne would necessarily imply. We parted, and in order to relieve myself from further proposals in this matter, and to show that my answer was final, I went off immediately to Paris, whither I had no previous intention of going, and I remained there until it was time to come back for the meeting of Parliament in October.'

V

Foreign Minister for the First Time, 1830–1841

TOWARDS THE CLOSE OF 1830 the Ministry of the Duke of Wellington was overthrown, and Lord Grey was commissioned to form a Government. The accession of Lord Grey to power enabled Palmerston to reach the goal of his ambition—the appointment of Secretary of State for Foreign Affairs.

This was the post that was dear to his heart, the only one in which he displayed ability of a very high order, and the subsequent record of his life is occupied very largely with the policy he thus inaugurated, and the results flowing from it.

Lord Palmerston was in favour of the great Reform Bill carried by Lord Grey, but he confined his efforts in that direction mainly to consistent voting in the right way. It was upon England's relations to the great diplomatic world that he kept his gaze steadily fixed. His letters and diaries enable us to follow very closely both his action and also his thoughts and opinions upon public affairs at this great crisis in English history.

'*Oct* 31, 1831. —After dinner yesterday I went and slept at the "Star and Garter" to have a cool night and a fresh ride in to-day, besides getting four hours' work at a paper I had to draw up free from one single interruption. People ought to be many months confined in London to know the value of even a few hours of fresh air and exercise. We are still without positive results at the Hague or Brussels, but Adair says that there is no doubt that the Belgians will accept by a large majority, but, like an African tribe, they insist upon having their palaver out, though every man has declared how he shall vote. We have not yet heard from the Hague since they knew of the sailing of our fleet. I think it will rather surprise them and bring them to reason. The riot at Bristol is unpleasant, and it seems that the officer in command of the troops made improper concessions to the mob, and agreed to withdraw his men because they were unpopular, leaving only a handful of one regiment which was in better odour with the people. Reinforcements have been sent, and the authority of the law will be maintained.

'*November* 1.—There has been a tremendous row at Bristol. All the public buildings of the town burnt, besides many private houses, and three hundred of the mob killed or wounded by the sabres of the cavalry. A proclamation will be issued to-morrow, calling on all persons to assist in maintaining the peace, and all requisite measures of vigour will be taken.

'*November* 5.—Five of the leaders of Monday's meeting had an interview with Melbourne, who told them that their assembly would be illegal, seditious, and possibly treasonable. He had no advice to give them. The Government would take all necessary measures for preserving the peace. It is quite a godsend to Melbourne to have an important affair in his hands. It rouses him wonderfully, and his activity is always in proportion to the urgency of the case.

'*November* 8.—I do not regret that the meeting was put off. Prevention is always better than cure, and when we can prevent disturbance, it is always right to do so; 'ce qui est différé est perdu,' is a much truer maxim than the contrary. The only good effect of cutting down some hundreds of vagabonds, at the price of many broken heads of respectable persons, and the burning of many honest men's houses, would have been to convince the rogues that the law and the Government are too strong for them, and if we have succeeded in inspiring that conviction by other means, why, so much the better. I take it they did not much relish the awkward words "sedition" and "high treason." The Government mean to use their influence to prevent the formation of these unions in various parts of the country. There were quantities of special constables sworn in yesterday. This let free the whole of the regular police to act against the mob in a body, if there had been need.

'*November* 16.—At last you may wish me joy. This morning, between two and three, we signed, sealed, and delivered six copies of the treaty of friendship and acknowledgment between the five Powers and Leopold, thus virtually and substantially settling this long-pending and complicated affair, for, Belgium being now constituted and placed under the guarantee of the five Powers, the Dutch King may sulk if he will ; but he can no longer endanger the peace of Europe, since all the five would be equally bound to resist him, and his only hopes were placed in the possibility of a division among them. Leopold had instructed Van de Weyer to obtain the promise of an acknowledgment before he signified his acceptance. Van de Weyer has now obtained actual acknowledgment, which is more. Leopold's acceptance was couched in doleful terms of complaint and reproach, and Talleyrand said it was an acceptance *dure et simple* instead of what we had asked for, *pure et simple*. We signed also between the four Powers and Van de Weyer an agreement to serve as the basis of a Convention about the fortresses, subject to confirmation by Leopold, from whom Van de Weyer had no instructions on this head. We consent to the demolition of Menin, Ath, Mons, Philippeville, and Marienbourg—preserving the citadel of Tournay and Charleroi, which France wanted to demolish, and demolishing Philippeville and Marienbourg, which they wanted to preserve. But the two former are useful for the defence of Belgium, and by demolishing the two others we shall destroy the motive which makes France so anxious to get possession of the nook of territory in which they stand. In signing this agreement, which was dated subsequently to the treaty, Van de Weyer signed second by virtue of alphabetical precedence, and he looked as pleased as if he had been made a prince himself. I suspect he will go back forthwith and become Minister of Foreign Affairs, and a very good one he will make. There was a doubt at one time last night whether all the things could be got ready in time to sign, and I said to Wessemberg that perhaps we should have to put it off till to-day. "No," said he, "old Talleyrand won't quit this roof without signing; his orders to his stockbroker are all given, and he must have the treaty signed before to-morrow morning." By-the-by, Talleyrand has lost a large sum lately at Paris, by a man whom he employed in these kinds of transactions, to buy and sell, not in Talleyrand's name, but in his own. This agent, getting into difficulties, has contended that what stands in his own name belongs to himself, and it will be hard, they say, to prove the contrary. To-day Lieven and Talleyrand and I have a little trio upon Greece.

'*November* 17.—Sebastiani is delighted at the idea of our treaty (the Belgian Treaty), and he said that it would give such a security to the peace of Europe that France would be able to disband a hundred thousand men at least, and that they would not have occasion to avail themselves of the law for mobilising the National Guard. They will, moreover, agree to some tolerable arrangement for a mutual right of search on the African coast to put an end to the slave trade. This will be popular here both with the saints and West Indians. We do not despair either of getting them to consent to some relaxation of their commercial codes, so as to let in our commodities upon a fairer footing.

'*November* 28.—Reform difficulties in the Cabinet. Grey and Althorp stick steadily to their point. The rest all have each their own objections, but it seldom happens that more than two or three concur in the importance of any one proposition, and thus are beaten in detail. We have ascertained the number of voters the £10 qualification will give in some of the large places—Birmingham 4,450, Manchester 22,639, Leeds 6,683, Liverpool 14,127, Bradford 1,083, Sheffield 4,575.

'*December* 3.—The French Minister has had instructions to make strong representations about Poland. The weight of Russian vengeance is to fall unmitigated upon Lithuania and the other Polish provinces incorporated with Russia. Siberia and confiscation, and deprivation even of the few privileges the people possessed, are to be the order of the day for those unfortunate districts. This is the course in despotic countries. First the people are goaded to rebellion by grievances unredressed, and then those grievances are increased tenfold to punish them for not having been contented.

'*December* 31.—My day was not an idle one, for, having left the office only at three in the morning the night before, I had, before the Cabinet at one, to write an important despatch to Vienna, to hear Czartorynski's account of the whole Polish war; and to discuss with Ompteda all the squabbles of the German Diet. After the Cabinet I had to see Van de Weyer, Lieven, Bulow, Esterhazy, and Wessemberg upon various different subjects, and afterwards to send off messengers with despatches and private letters to Vienna, Berlin, Paris, and Brussels. However, I contrived to get it all done by about two this morning—and now, for my consolation,

I have staring me in the face thirteen boxes full of papers, which ought all to be read forthwith, and which have come to me since yesterday morning … As to the French, I was quite right in maintaining that, if we only held our ground, the French fury would end in bluster, and would not lead to any unpleasant results. Talleyrand is quite come round upon that subject, swears that so far from having blown the coals, as we happen to know he did, he always preached temper and moderation, and, instead of demanding the demolition of God knows how many fortresses if we wish to avoid war, he hopes we will write him a civil not; assuring him that the Convention has nothing in it hostile to France.'

The partition of the districts of the Low Countries between Belgium and Holland, the diplomatic matter referred to in the above extracts, occupied Lord Palmerston and the representatives of foreign Powers much at this time, and the business was not finally settled till 1839.

The kingdom of Holland as constituted, mainly by the influence of England, in 1814–15 was dissolved, and the independence of Belgium under King Leopold secured and guaranteed. The details of the settlement are too intricate and too extensive to be dealt with here, but the treaty signed in 1831 was the first, and has so far been one of the most lasting, of Palmerston's diplomatic triumphs. His second was the treaty known as the Quadruple Alliance, which linked England and France together in defence of constitutional government in Spain and Portugal. This was signed in London on April 22, 1834, and writing about it a few weeks later Palmerston said, 'This treaty was a capital hit, and all my own doing.'

Meanwhile in domestic affairs the passage of the Reform Bill was the all-absorbing interest. On a renewal of an Irish Coercion Bill, Lord Grey resigned, and Lord Melbourne, with whom Lord Palmerston had always been in close sympathy, succeeded to the first place in the Ministry. With a brief interruption while Sir Robert Peel's Government held office for a few months in 1834 and 1835, he remained for many years at the Foreign Office. King William was not unfriendly, as his predecessor had been, to Lord Palmerston, and he spoke with apparent hearty approval the Speech from the Throne, which in 1834 alluded to the Slavery Abolition Bill, stating that the manner in which that measure had been received throughout the Colonies, and the progress made in carrying it into effect in Jamaica, 'afforded just grounds for the happiest results.'

Three years later civil war broke out in Spain. The Tories supported, while the Whigs steadily discountenanced Don Carlos, the man of whom Palmerston said, 'He is a mere pretender, seeking a throne he never sat on, invading and carrying civil war into a country to which he had no claim.' Lord Palmerston was attacked for allowing a British Legion, several thousand men in number, to take part in the struggle, and defended his policy in speeches of great vigour and force. 'Did not history tell us,' he said, 'that it was in the character of the Spanish people to be more reckless of the shedding of blood than any other nation in Europe? And was it for those who had seen the arms of England aided by the ruthless guerillas to urge this part of the Spanish character as a reason for refusing them their co-operation? He trusted that one of the first fruits of the Spanish regeneration through the means of a free constitution would be the creation of a public opinion tending to correct these faults in the national character ... However skilfully the question might be disguised, it involved nothing less than the alternative whether England should continue to fulfil her engagement to the Queen of Spain, or disgracefully abandon an ally she had pledged herself to succour.

'With respect to the assertion that the moral influence of England has declined since I came into office, I think it rather inconsistent with the hosts of assailants which the same policy has called up with regard to Belgium, Portugal, and Spain. It is rather surprising that our Government should obtain so much countenance and respect from foreign countries as to be made the arbiter of their disputes; and when we find two great naval Powers like France and America—each of them in former times opposed to us in war, and each of them supposed to be our rivals in the arts of peace as well as in the pursuit of war—when we find them conceding to us the adjustment of their differences, I think I may appeal with confidence to that single fact in reply, and say that whatever is the estimate formed of us by our opponents, France and America at least, do not seem persuaded that our moral influence has sunk to so low a state.'

When France demanded the expulsion of French political refugees from Switzerland he replied: 'If I might presume to give advice to the

Swiss in such a case it would be that the course to be pursued under the circumstances, and conformably with the good understanding that ought to prevail betwixt neighbouring States, would be that any persons who are really guilty of such practices (as conspiring against the Government of France) should be requested to leave the country, the shelter of which they have abused.'

He defended the part he had taken in the Quadruple Alliance, and the allegation that we had reduced Spain, one of the Powers that made the treaty, to weakness, was denied. Of her and of Portugal he said: 'Portugal, not yet recovered from the fierce struggle in the midst of which she has acquired her free institutions, is now in that situation in which she must be looked upon as one of the substantive Powers of Europe. Spain holds out to us a fair and legitimate hope that she may yet become what she has been in former times—a flourishing and even a formidable Power among the European kingdoms.'

It was in this year also that William IV died and Queen Victoria was called, when a girl of eighteen, to the throne. Palmerston was present at the formal beginnings of the new reign, and has left on record his impressions:

'*June* 20, 1837.—The poor King (William IV) was released from his sufferings at an early hour this morning. The Privy Council met this morning at Kensington, and was most numerously attended. The Queen went through her task to-day with great dignity and self-possession. One saw that she felt much inward emotion, but it was fully controlled. Her articulation was particularly good, and her voice remarkably pleasing. To-day and to-morrow the two Houses do nothing but take the oaths. On Thursday there will be a message, as usual in such cases, to the two Houses, and an address in reply.

'*June* 27.—To-day the Queen received the addresses of the House of Commons, and afterwards the Foreign Ministers. They were introduced one by one. Nothing could be better than her manner of receiving them; it was easy and dignified and gracious.'

In the following year England had to keep a tight hand both on Mehemet Ali in Egypt and on the Porte. Affairs were already tending in the direction that led ultimately to the Crimean War. Lord Palmerston writes: 'In regard to the Turks themselves, may I venture to observe that the genius of their manners and conversation is that of yielding everything at first? They begin by saying "Good; Yes," but when you come to the matter in question and to its details, you will find all those fine expressions mean nothing. Like all people in a feeble position, they respect you according to their opinion of your *force*. If, however, you wish that force to have a permanent influence and to be unaccompanied by dislike, you must blend its exercise with justice; and if you wish to arrive at a quick result through all that ambuscade of intrigues and doubts and fears and prejudices which will be sure to be secretly formed against it, you must tell the Turk what he is to do, why he is to do it, when he is to do it, and show him that you only ask quietly and reasonably what you have a right to demand. In this way and in this way alone, you will do business with him, If he sees you act thus he will not only agree with you, but rely upon you.'

On French affairs Lord Palmerston writes, November 1840:

'I hope no one will believe that there exists at present in France that danger of internal revolution and of external war which the French Government, to serve its own diplomatic purposes, endeavours to represent. There is, no doubt, a large party among the leading politicians in France who have long contemplated the establishment of a virtually, if not actually, independent State in Egypt and Syria, under the direct protection and influence of France, and that party feel great disappointment and resentment at finding their schemes in this respect baffled. But that party will not revenge themselves on the four Powers by making a revolution in France, and they are enlightened enough to see that France cannot revenge herself by making war against the four Powers, who are much stronger than she is. The late French Government, in order to intimidate the four Powers, raised a war-cry in France, and excited the nation by asserting that France had been insulted and deceived, and when a government begins the work of agitation it cannot fail of being successful. But the King of the French co-operated with his Minister in this agitation, and therefore must have felt an inward conviction that the excitement could be controlled, if it should not produce the desired effect. It was, in fact, certain that when the stimulating action of the Government should cease to act, the excitement created by that action would gradually die away, and this is beginning already to be seen, as is proved by the immense and unexpectedly large majority in favour of the Government in the election of the Speaker. The French Government, who wish to have the double advantage of the reality of strength at home and of the character of weakness abroad, say that this division is no test of the relative strength of parties on the question of peace and war, but it surely must be an indication that the peace party is much the stronger, although the majority may vary ... Even had M. Thiers remained Minister, France could not have made war before the beginning of next summer, because France would not have had 300,000 men disposable for aggressive war till new levies had been raised, which could not have been completed till then, and even that amount of force would have been considerably inferior in number and composition to the force which Germany could bring into the field. But we may be sure that there is in France an immense mass of persons possessed of property and engaged in pursuits of industry who are decidedly adverse to unnecessary war, and determined to oppose revolution, and although those persons have not hitherto come prominently forward, yet their voice would have made itself heard, when the question of peace or unprovoked war came practically to be discussed. With regard to internal revolution, there is undoubtedly in France a large floating mass of republicans and anarchists, ready at any moment to make a disturbance if there was no strong power to resist them; but the persons who would lose by convulsions are infinitely more numerous, and the National Guard of Paris, consisting of 60,000 men, are chiefly persons of this description, and are understood to be decidedly for internal order and for external peace.

'It is very natural that the French Government, after having failed to extort concessions on the Turkish question, by menaces of foreign war, should now endeavour to obtain those concessions by appealing to fears of another kind, and should say that such concessions are necessary in order to prevent revolution in France; but I am sure that this appeal is not better founded than the other, and that a firm and resolute perseverance on the part of the four Powers in the measures which they have taken in hand will effect a settlement of the affairs of Turkey which will afford great additional security for the future peace of Europe without producing in the meantime either war with France or revolution in France. France and the rest of Europe are entirely different now from what they were in 1792.

The French nation is as much interested now to avoid further revolution as it was interested then in ridding itself by any means of the enormous and intolerable abuses which then existed. France then imagined she had much to gain by foreign war. France now knows she has everything to lose by foreign war. Europe then (at least the Continental States) had also a strong desire to get rid of innumerable abuses which pressed heavily upon the people of all countries. Those abuses have now in general been removed. The people in many parts of Germany have been admitted, more or less, to a share in the management of their own affairs. A German feeling and a spirit of nationality has sprung up among all the German people, and the Germans, instead of receiving the French as liberators, as many of them did in 1792 and 1793, would now rise as one man to repel a hateful invasion. On all these grounds I am convinced that the appeals made to us by the King of the French upon the score of the danger of revolution in France unless concessions are made to the French Government have no foundation in truth, and are only exertions of skilful diplomacy.'

He was able at intervals to enjoy the quiet of his beautiful home in Hampshire.

The Foreign Minister writes from Broadlands (March 1841):

'We are here alone, doing all sorts of country business, and trying to set straight a variety of things which have gone wrong under Holmes's neglect, and while I was too busy to attend to my own affairs. I have not much time to write, as it is late; and I have only just returned from John Day's (the trainer), where I have been to see Ilione and a filly I have there, and to look over Day's stable. I saw old Mrs Day, still well and glad to see an old friend. We have got a new gardener, who is a jewel of a man, an active, little fellow, very intelligent and zealous. Stewart was too tall to be worth anything. I am convinced by my observation of mankind that being about five-foot ten is a strong *prima facie* presumption against a man's intelligence and activity of mind.'

In May, 1841, Lord Palmerston wrote to his brother William:

'We have had another May crisis. This month has been the one which is dangerous to administrations. Huskisson and the rest of us left the Duke's Government in May, 1828; and I think most of the resignations that have happened in Lord Grey's time and in Melbourne's have taken place in May.

We doubted long whether we should resign or dissolve, but the country has taken our part so decidedly that we have determined to dissolve. There remains some routine business to get through before the session can be closed, and I imagine the dissolution will take place in about three weeks. It is not easy to foresee the result of a general election, but I think we shall increase our majority. The country is with us, and the Tory party cannot make the same great efforts all over the country at a general election which they can at a single place upon one particular vacancy. The Anti-Slavery cry has certainly failed. The Poor Law cry is failing also, while on the other hand, the Corn Law and Free Trade cries are telling immensely. At one time we thought that the Tories might have tried to prevent us from dissolving in order to compel us to resign instead. But such a course would not suit the views and opinions of the Duke or of Peel. It would be too factious, and too openly hostile to the Crown and to the Prerogative to admit of its being adopted by either of them. I doubt not that many of the inferior men in the party wished it. Parliament will meet as soon as possible after the elections, some time in August, and do what may be left undone at the dissolution. But its meeting then will short.'

Events did not in this instance fully bear out Lord Palmerston's forecast. Defeated by a majority of one on a vote of want of confidence, proposed by Sir Robert Peel in June, 1841, Lord Melbourne dissolved Parliament, and in the new Parliament, on an amendment to the Address moved by Sir Robert Peel, was left in a minority of ninety-one. Melbourne at once resigned, and Peel formed the Government which, little as he then imagined, was to repeal the Corn Laws. Meanwhile Lord Palmerston, once again in opposition, watched the course of public affairs with the keenest interest.

VI

In Opposition and again at the Foreign Office, 1841–1851

AT THE CLOSE OF 1841 Sir Robert Peel was not only the foremost man in England, but one of the most powerful ministers of modern times. The finances of the nation had been allowed to fall behind. Great commercial reforms, supported by some of the ablest and most eloquent Englishmen, were steadily moving forward. Released from the stress of Foreign Office work, and keenly alive to the fact that the time had arrived when, if ever, he was to make it evident that he possessed qualities fitting him for the highest of all political posts, Lord Palmerston threw all his energy into the work of opposition. He gave further evidence of his power as a speaker, and his capacity for telling and convincing debate. From his correspondence at this time it is evident that he kept his eye upon most departments of the active life of the day.

'There is a storm getting up about the income tax, but I think Peel will carry it notwithstanding. Malmesbury said to me the other day: "Peel hit us a right-hander with his Corn Law, and a hard left-hander with his income tax, but this tax about timber is a regular facer. My father and grandfather have not touched a stick for forty years, and now I was thinking of doing some good with my elms and firs, when down comes Peel with his free importation of Canada timber, and my trees will not be worth a farthing."'

While voting with Lord John Russell in favour of a moderate fixed duty on corn, Palmerston seems very early to have reached the conviction that the abolition of all imposts of the kind was only a matter of time.

Near the end of the session of 1842 he made a vigorous attack upon the whole policy of the Government. Speaking of Lord Stanley, he said: 'The noble Lord made a very good off-hand speech, for no man is a better off-hand debater than the noble Lord. But off-hand debaters are sometimes apt to say whatever may come into their heads on the spur of the moment without stopping to consider, as they would do if they had time, whether what they are going to say is strictly consistent with the facts to which it applies. I remember to have heard of a celebrated minister of a foreign country, who lived about the middle of the last century, who was giving instructions to one of his agents as to the language he should hold in regard to the conduct of another Government. The agent, having listened to the instructions, ventured with great humility and very submissively to suggest that the language he was ordered to hold was not strictly consistent with fact, and might indeed be thought to be altogether at variance with fact. What was the minister's answer? "Never mind *that*! What in the world does that signify? It is a good thing to say and take care you say it." That minister would, I think, have made not a bad off-hand debater in this House.'

Palmerston proceeded to repel the charge levelled by Lord Stanley against the Government of which he had been a member, to the effect that their policy had been a restless meddling with the business of the world. 'So far,' he says, 'from having left embarrassments to our successors, we have bequeathed to them facilities. Why, what have they been doing since they came into office? They have been living upon our leavings. 'They have been subsisting upon the broken victuals which they found upon our table. They are like a band of men who have made a forcible entrance into a dwelling, and who sit down and carouse upon the provisions they found in the larder.'

In 1844 he writes to his brother: 'I send you "Coningsby," well worth reading and admirably written; the characters are many of them perfect portraits. You will recognise Croker in Rigby, Lord Hertford in Monmouth, Lowther in Eskdale, Irving in Ormsby, Madame Zichy in Lucretia, but not Lady Strachan in Countess Colonna, though the character is evidently meant to fill her place in the family party. Sidonia is, I suppose, meant as a sort of type of the author himself, and Henry Sidney is Lord John Manners.'

In this year Palmerston again travelled on the Continent, visiting Berlin and Wiesbaden and Dresden. 'At Berlin we dined with the King, the Prince of Prussia, Prince Charles and Bülow, and nothing could be more courteous than the Royal family were. They are really a very remarkable family and would be distinguished persons in any rank of life. The King is a man of much acquirements, much natural talent, and enlightened views, and there can be no doubt that under his reign Prussia will make great and rapid advance in improvement of every kind. The greater part of the nobility in Prussia spend most of the year on their estates, and do not live much at Berlin. The King makes up for this by surrounding himself with men of science, literature, and art, and Prussia is accordingly making great progress in intellectual development. The late King endeavoured to keep everything stationary and stagnant; the present King is all for improvement. He was a great patron of Schinkel, the architect, and is himself full of taste that way, and he is going to pull down an ugly church in the great square before the old palace, and to build in its stead a Campo Santo for the Royal family, to be ornamented in the inside with frescoes, for which Cornelius is making a magnificent design ... Nature has not been bountiful to Prussia, at least to the district round Berlin, as regards soil and perhaps climate; but she has been more liberal as to mental endowments, and one cannot visit the country without being struck with the great intellectual activity which shows itself in all classes. There is scarcely a man in the country who cannot read and write. In short, Prussia is taking the lead in German civilisation; and as Austria has gone to sleep, and it will be long before she wakes, Prussia has a fine career open to her for many years to come. One is the more struck with the activity of the people in these parts of Germany in intellectual development because they are so far behind in most of the mechanical arts connected with the habits of domestic life. In a country where the winters are very severe there is not such a thing as a window-shutter to be seen, doors and windows never shut, locks are such as were made in England a century and a half ago, and all things of this kind are still a hundred years behind what are seen with us now. To be sure, their palaces are magnificent but that is characteristic of imperfect civilisation. The middle ages and half civilised countries have combined splendid palaces with comfortless habitations for private individuals; not, however, that the German houses are uncomfortable, for we have met everywhere with very good inns.

Palmerston's foreign travels had not enamoured him of foreign tariffs. In 1845, speaking in the House of Commons, he asked: 'Is the state of our commercial relations with foreign countries a reason why we should maintain the system of Protection? Some people say it is. Some gentlemen argue that Free Trade might do very well if it were practised by all nations, but that one-sided Free Trade will not do; that our example will not be followed, and that this system, not being mutual and reciprocal, will be an injury to ourselves and an advantage to other nations. Now, I hold this to be just as great a fallacy as the other. For what is the effect of mutually hostile tariffs between ourselves and other countries? Take any foreign country—take France, for instance. The high tariffs of France and of England are alike injurious to both countries. Our high tariff against French commodities is an injury to ourselves as consumers and to the French as producers; while the high tariff of France against British commodities is an injury to the French consumers as well as to the English producers. Here then is an inconvenience on both sides of the water.'

Lord Palmerston was ever anxious that his activity in the interests of England should not be dubbed 'warlike interference,' and in this connection a letter from Mr Disraeli, written from Paris in the year 1845, possesses special value. It was docketed by Lord Palmerston: 'Mr Disraeli— Conversations with the King of the French and M. Guizot about prospect of my return to the Foreign Office.' The letter runs as follow:

'M. Guizot invited me to a private conversation on the intelligence which had arrived from London. In some casual talk previously with the Duc Decazes, I had ascertained that it was M. Guizot's opinion that Sir R. Peel would be restored to power "dans une quinzaine." M. Guizot did not express this opinion to me, but he elicited mine, that the return of Sir R. Peel, assuming the supposed causes of his retirement to be correct, was highly improbable. Yesterday the King, whom I had had the honour to see during the throes of the last fortnight, in which, though anxious, he seemed confident as to Peel's triumph, sent for me to St Cloud. I found his Majesty grave and calm, more ready to listen than to talk, very consecutive and keeping to the point. His Majesty told me that M. Guizot had mentioned in the morning at the Council that he had seen me on the previous eve. His Majesty's belief in Peel had evaporated; he repeated, more than once, that Guizot was disabused of his idea that Peel would return; that every resignation weakened a man, and was almost as silly a thing as frequent Cabinet Councils. After some conversation on this head—the probable materials of the new Ministry—the King, assuming that there would be a Whig Government, spoke to me very much of your Lordship's accession to office. Your Lordship is doubtless aware of the apprehensions which the people of this country entertain on that subject, and therefore I will not dwell on them. Your Lordship is a person of too great experience and of too great a mind either to exaggerate or depreciate the importance of such circumstances. In the present instance, being not unfamiliar with the subject, it was in my power to discuss it in all its bearings, and to make those representations to the King and enter into those explanations and details which were desirable. I impressed on his Majesty with delicacy, but with reserve, that your Lordship was our first Foreign Minister who had taken the French intimacy as an avowed element of our national policy, and that the original want of cordiality had not been manifested by you. That from your character you required frankness and decision from those with whom you co-operated, and that, if these qualities were not want-ing on the part of the French Government, I felt sure that your Lordship would never take a litigious view of the policy of France, but rather would assist in any fair development of its influence which had for its object to popularise the Throne and satisfy the public. There followed on the part of the King some explanations of Spanish and Egyptian affairs, which I had heard from him on other occasions, but which were now expressed with gravity and much earnestness. This conversation lasted about half an hour, when the King, rising, said: "We must not lose all this pretty music" (there was a concert in an adjoining room, though only the Court present), "and I must say a word to one or two persons, but do not go, as I wish to speak to you again." Accordingly, about 10.30, the concert having finished, his Majesty approached me and invited me to follow him into his Cabinet. He said, the moment we were seated: "What you have said of Lord Palmerston has given me much pleasure. I have been thinking of it. I feel also persuaded that Peel cannot be brought back again in triumph, and, if he were to return, he is no longer the same man. I will not deny I regret Lord Aberdeen. But if Lord Palmerston will enter his administration without 'rancune' and with a friendly disposition, all may be well. I consider that affairs are very serious. It is not isolated questions now. Isolated questions settle themselves. Or even America, the same. It is the state of the Continent that occupies me." His Majesty then entered, at great length, on this subject. I perceived that the state of Germany disquiets him; and that he believes that a vast revolutionary movement in Central Europe is not to be avoided. Approaching midnight, his Majesty dismissed me.'

Mr Disraeli then suggests to Lord Palmerston that some step should be taken to rid the French of their distrust of him. 'Had you made your projected visit to Paris and become known to these impressionable people, all would have been right ... On the meeting of Parliament, under circumstances which render developments of policy on the part of a government not unusual, it would not be difficult to arrange something which would elicit a satisfactory answer. I am sure I should be very happy to assist you in this respect if Parliament be summoned speedily, otherwise I do not think I shall be tempted to quit this agreeable residence; especially as the great object of my political life is now achieved.'

The subject of Disraeli's interesting and courteous letter was alluded to by Lord Palmerston in a speech in the House of Commons, in reply to some accusations against him as possessing warlike tendencies:

'I am sure it is not to be believed for an instant that I do not attach the greatest importance to the maintenance, not merely of peace with all foreign countries, but of the most friendly relations with those leading Powers and States of the world with which serious differences would be attended with the most inconvenience. As to peace, I succeeded, as the organ of Lord Grey's and Lord Melbourne's Governments, in preserving it unbroken during ten years of great and extraordinary difficulty; and if now and then it unavoidably happened during that period of time that, in pursuing the course of policy which seemed the best for British interests, we thwarted the views of this and that foreign Power, and rendered them for the moment less friendly, I think I could prove that, in every case, the object which we were pursuing was of sufficient importance to make it worth our while to submit to such temporary inconveniences.

'There never was indeed, during those ten years, any real danger of war, except on three occasions; and on each of these occasions the course pursued by the British Government prevented war. The first occasion was just after the accession of the King of the French, when Austria, Russia, and Prussia were disposed and preparing to attack Franc; and when the attitude assumed by the British Government prevented a rupture. The second was when England and France united by a convention to wrest the citadel of Antwerp from the Dutch, and to deliver it over to the King of the Belgians. If England had not been joined with France Antwerp would have remained with the Dutch, and the attempt to take it would have led to a war in Europe. The third occasion was when Mehemet Ali's army occupied Syria and when he was constantly threatening to declare himself independent, and to march upon Constantinople; while Russia, on the one hand, asserted that if he did so she would occupy Constantinople, and, on the other hand, France announced that if Russia did so, she, France, would force the Dardanelles.

'The Treaty of July, 1840, proposed and brought about by the British Government, and the operations in execution of that treaty, put an end to that danger, and, notwithstanding what has been often said to the contrary, the real danger of war, as arising out of the affairs of Syria, was put an end to, and not created, by the Treaty of 1840. 1 am well aware, however, that some persons, both at home and abroad, have imbibed the notion that I am more indifferent than I ought to be as to running the risk of war. This impression abroad is founded on an entire mistake, but is by some sincerely felt, and, being sincere, would soon yield to the evidence of contradictory facts. At home that impression has been industriously propagated to a limited extent, partly by the legitimate attacks of political opponents, partly by a like cabal in our own ranks. These parties wanted to attack me, and were obliged to accuse me of something. They could not charge me with failure, because we had succeeded in all our undertakings, whether in Portugal, Spain, Belgium, Syria, China, or elsewhere. They could not charge me with having involved the country in war, because in fact we had maintained peace; and the only thing which was left for them to say was that my policy had a tendency to produce war, and I suppose they would argue that it was quite wrong and against all rule that it did not do so. But, notwithstanding what may have been said on this matter, the transaction which has by some been the most criticised in this respect, namely, the Treaty of 1840, and the operations connected with it, were entirely approved by the leaders of the then Opposition, who, so far from feeling any disposition to favour me, had always made a determined run at the foreign policy of the Whig Government. The Duke of Wellington, at the opening or the session of 1841, said in the House of Lords that he entirely approved our policy in that transaction, and could not find that any fault had been committed by us in working it out; and I happen to know that Sir Robert Peel expressed to the Representative of one of the German Powers, parties to the alliance, his entire approval of our course, while Lord Aberdeen said to one of them that the course I had taken in that affair made him forgive me many things of former years which he had thought he never should have forgiven.'

The year 1846 saw the fall of Sir Robert Peel's Government. The Prime Minister's conversion to the views of Cobden and Bright on the subject of the Corn Laws led to their total abolition. It also led to the defection of a body of his supporters under the leadership of Lord Stanley. On the same night in which the House of Lords read the Corn Laws Repeal Bill a third time, Sir Robert Peel was defeated in the Commons on the continuance of a bill to protect life and property in Ireland. Peel at once resigned, Lord John Russell became Prime Minister, and Lord Palmerston occupied his post at the Foreign Office for the third time.

Before entering into harness Lord Palmerston passed a month in Ireland, and the following year, when the potato disease began to assume disastrous dimensions in that country, he was busy arranging for the comfort of those who had left Ireland for richer lands. He was always most generous and thoughtful for all the people on his Irish estates.

In 1847, the Irish people had risen in number to over double what the soil could support except for the introduction of the potato; and hence with the failure of that plant came dismay and death. Along the St Lawrence and on many spots on the eastern coast of the United States are still pointed out the places where the hospitals were erected to shelter and isolate the wretched persons who came over from Ireland by the hundred and by the thousand, smitten with fever. There on the shores of the promised land very many died, victims of their improvident and thriftless habits, and of resistance to the introduction among them at home of better agriculture, and that improvement which always appears to the imagination of the unmixed Celt as an alien garb to fetter his limbs.

At this time a contract was made for the voluntary emigration of some of the poor from his land in the County Sligo, and Lord Palmerston wrote that if the terms were not sufficient to treat his people well, to rescind the terms, and put in a higher tender to enable them to get the best entertainment on board the ships. 'Let every man and woman,' he wrote, 'have a hot tumbler of the best Jamaica rum-punch after dinner on Sundays or oftener.' But these good intentions, though fully appreciated by the travellers, were not quite satisfactory to some of their friends. Lord Palmerston had soon to write: 'The clergy write to me that I am doing away the good effected by Father Mathew among the people. You will therefore sell the rum you have taken on board for the punch, on arrival at Quebec, and let every man, woman, and child have a cup of hot coffee with a biscuit every day after dinner.' Ten pounds sterling were given to each captain of ships conveying any of Lord Palmerston's people, to induce the officer to be kind to them, and some brandy and port wine, as well for the use of the passengers if sick, as for the enjoyment of the skipper.

His Irish anxieties in 1847 alternated in his mind with a foreign matter which would not nowadays come home so much to the mind of an English minister. This was the question of the Spanish Marriages on which there are volumes of correspondence by Lord Palmerston, but it will not be necessary to say much about them here. It seems almost strange to us that we should have feared so much as we then did the extension of French influence in Spain, through the family intrigues and dynastic ambition of the Bourbons. That Guizot and Louis Philippe should plan a marriage for the Queen of Spain which should ultimately turn out to the benefit of the French Bourbons was gall and wormwood to British ministers and diplomatists. We think now that the influence that might have been so acquired was not of a formidable character, but Guizot's plans were fought against as actively as if the task were that of again freeing Madrid from a French army.

Marshal Narvaez had established a military despotism, and Lord Palmerston writes in September, 1847:

'The fight between Narvaez and the interests of Spain and England is still going on, but I hope we shall win, though no doubt Narvaez is well furnished by Louis Philippe and Christina with the sinews of war. But the race is not always to the swiftest, nor the victory to him who has most money. Espartero is wisely waiting to see how things turn out, and will not go to Spain. They want to shelve him by making him Ambassador Extraordinary here; and extraordinary he would be, as he would have nothing to do, because they propose him to be in addition to Isturitz, and it would be quite the old story of John doing nothing and Tom helping him. Espartero can converse in no language but his impure Castilian, and few ministers can discuss affairs with him in that dialect of human speech. Metternich is gone foolish, but I think we shall be able to stop him, and France must go with us in Italian affairs. Metternich thinks he has her in his pocket, because he has had promises from Louis Philippe and Guizot, but public opinion in France must be stronger than the King and his minister, and as they broke their word to us last year about Spain, so will they be compelled to break their word this year to Metternich about Italy. I do not fear war out of any of these matters. As to the defence of this country, we are going to take this matter up, and I hesitate not to say that we should be guilty of treason to the country if we allowed things to remain as they are, and the United Kingdom and its foreign possessions to be as defenceless as at present. Fortifications are making and will be completed to protect the dockyards from surprise. Harbours will be constructed where steamers can lie, ready to intercept and repel attacking squadrons. But all naval prevention is uncertain, and in spite of every defensive precaution, dark nights, foggy days, storms, accidents, blunders, may enable an enemy to land 20,000 or 30,000 men on our coast, either in England or in Ireland, or in both. The only defence that can be relied upon against an attack of armed men is an equal or superior body of armed men. Our regular army cannot furnish us with such defence. We have some 50,000 or 60,000 men on paper in the United Kingdom including depots, skeleton battalions, recruits just raised, and invalids about to be discharged. We could not out of this motley mass collect *an army* of 20,000 either in England or in Ireland, to meet 20,000 or 30,000 French or Russians (and we might have to deal with both) landed on our shores. We cannot increase our regular army to the requisite amount because it would be too expensive to do so. The only way to provide for such a contingent emergency is to have a force which shall acquire a certain degree of organisation, training, and discipline in time of peace, so as to be moderately efficient immediately on the breaking out of war; but which during peace, and when not wanted for actual service, shall cost us as little as possible. The militia is such a force, being trained in peace for only one month in the year. It costs about one quarter of what an equal number of regulars in pay all the year round would cost, and yet in a couple of years it would acquire, by the month's training, military habits enough to make it fit to be mixed up with troops of the line at the outbreak of a war, especially if it contained a good infusion of half-pay officers. The plan is to amend the Act of 1802, which fixed the number of men to be raised by each county. The increase of population would entitle us to fix the number at 100,000 for this island, and 40,000 for Ireland, and if I was to decide, that should be the amount of our reserve force, and it should all be organised, regimented, officered, clothed, armed, equipped, and trained.'

In February, 1848, the London papers appeared with the headings in largest type:

'Abdication of Louis Philippe—The Count of Paris is King—The Duke of Nemours as Regent is rejected—The Royal Family have left Paris—A Provincial Government is installed, composed of Lamartine, Ledru Rollin, Odilon Barrot, Marie Arago, Garnier Pages, Louis Blanc.'

A letter to Lord Palmerston from Paris said: 'Events have succeeded each other within the last twenty-four hours with a rapidity unexampled in any previous revolution, and the greatest changes have been produced by the most unexpected incidents. At the time I wrote yesterday there seemed to be every reason to suppose the population of Paris had received for the moment the full satisfaction they desired in the dismissal of the ministers, obtained as it had been by the National Guard demanding it as the price of their allegiance. You will perceive how much this had already shaken the fabric of national government, and how much this overt act of the National Guard had altered the character of the demonstration. This demonstration on the Monday, though very numerous, was perfectly peaceable whenever there were large masses collected, and only mischievous in small bands in different parts of the town. The great mistake committed by the Government at this period of the affair was that, after having announced their intention to call out the National Guard on Monday morning, they recalled that order, and it was only at dusk, and under the apprehension that those who had hitherto been only idle spectators might at night take to plunder, that the roll-call beat. The National Guard, disgusted with the distrust which had been shown, and the nature of the service alone confided to them, assembled but partially, and the next morning, when they were again called out, the political feeling soon showed itself in a manner which made it evident that no reliance could be placed upon them by the Government. Several legions marched to the Tuileries, and deputations from the officers of the *arrondissements* met them there, and the King became convinced that he had no alternative but to dismiss his ministers, and he summoned Count Mole. The announcement of the dissolution of the Guixot Cabinet was received with enthusiasm; the funds at once rose ½ per cent; many of the barricades were destroyed by the people who had raised them; a considerable portion of Paris was spontaneously illuminated. Mobs proceeded to the houses of M. Thiers, M. Odilon Barrot, and others, cheering under the windows, as might occur in London before the residences of any popular leaders upon a similar occasion. Up to this moment all appeared calculated to inspire hope that, the real cause of the discontent being removed, the town would to-day resume its tranquillity, when an unexpected incident or casualty, as it would almost seem, completely changed the face of affairs, and produced events the effects of which, it is impossible not to foresee, will long be felt throughout Europe. A mob of about a hundred and fifty, many of them armed, were followed by a curious crowd, and these had been proceeding in different directions requiring that the houses should be illuminated. They had succeeded in this at the Ministère de la Justice, as I am told, and intended to require the same at the Ministère des Affaires Etrangères, from which M. Guizot is said to have already removed himself. Upon the arrival of the crowd before the hotel, a single shot, by whom fired will, perhaps, never be ascertained, but coming from the direction of the garden wall, broke the leg of the horse on which the major commanding the detachment of the 14th Regiment of the Line was mounted. He immediately, without the slightest notice, gave an order to fire a volley into the crowd, which had been collected before the hotel. It is, stated that no less than fifty-two people, many of them women and children, were killed or wounded. An English gentleman, Mr Henry Fitzroy, who was walking quietly along on the other side of the Boulevards, told me that men fell on each side of him. The crowd immediately dispersed into the different quartiers of Paris from which they had been collected, shouting vengeance and treachery. The barricades were reconstructed, new ones were formed in various parts of Paris, and when morning came it found the whole population in the greatest state of exasperation. Many of the middle classes, who had hitherto remained quiet, became indignant at that which at first sight was supposed to have been a massacre ordered by superior authority.

'Some attributed it to M. Guizot, who, however, I have reason to believe, had nothing whatever to do with it, and was not even there. Others unfortunately openly attributed treachery to the King. From the very beginning of these disastrous affairs the has been that, as the offence was taken at the tone of the King's Speech, and as it was generally believed that the words were his own, the disposition has been to attribute every unpopular act to him personally, and this incident occurring in the interval after the dismissal of his ministers, the exasperation against the King increased, and rendered any arrangement difficult. In the course of the night the Count Mole had announced that the time was passed when it was possible for him to be of service to the King, and that nothing remained for him but to send for M. Thiers and M. Odilon Barrot. A new Ministry was announced this morning. It appears that the result of the affray has been to ensure a manifestation of the troops of the Line, that they did not approve of that which was called the massacre committed by the 14th Regiment. The sympathies of the troops had already been suspected greatly, and the withdrawal of the regular troops from Paris was caused by the necessity of preserving some appearance of discipline. The last conflict was this morning at a *corps de garde*, when the municipal guard were summoned to surrender the post by the people, and, refusing to do it, firing commenced on both sides; several were killed, the post carried, and plundered. I have just heard that the disposition shown by the people has led to the abdication of the King in favour of the Comte de Paris, under the regency of the Duchess of Orleans. King Louis Philippe is said to have left Paris an hour since.'

Lord Palmerston sent English steam packets to Havre and Cherbourg 'for the purpose of affording to the French King and Queen the means of escape if they should be in a condition to avail themselves thereof.' He soon after received news that they were at Havre, and writes stating the arrangement made for securing the escape of the King and Queen, and says at the same time that the success of these arrangements essentially depends on the strictest secrecy being observed as to the place of concealment of their Majesties. His correspondent had written from Havre: 'The King is at Trouville in disguise, and in most friendly hands. The Queen is at Honfleur, and quite safe. When the storm which has now been raging for twelve hours abates, the King is to embark at Trouville with the ebb tide, which will float him out of the Seine, and when the fishing boat in which he is to leave Trouville reaches Cape de Héve, a signal is to be made to the captain of our express steamer, who will leave Havre, and will be under the cape and out of sight of this place. He is to go under gentle steam until the fishing boat boards him. The captain thinks with me that if this simple operation be carried out by the Trouville boat, that the manoeuvre will be carried out without observation.'

Lord Palmerston writes on March 3, 1848: 'The King and Queen of the French landed this morning at Newhaven. General Dumas says that till the morning after their arrival at Dreux the King and the Queen imagined that the Comte de Paris had succeeded to the throne, and that the Duchess of Orleans had been declared regent; that when they heard that a Republic and Provisional Government had been declared, they thought it unsafe to remain at Dreux, and that they then separated in order to go by different roads to Honfleur, where they were to meet at a small house belonging to General Dumas. At that house they remained for some days. The King remained two or three days at Trouville, but the weather was too stormy to allow of his departure as arranged. In the meantime the people of Trouville found out who he was, and their demonstrations of attachment became inconvenient. He therefore returned to Honfleur, and the arrangements were altered. Yesterday evening at seven o'clock the King and Queen and General Dumas came to the ferry-boat which plies between Havre and Honfleur, and were met by the Vice-Consul, who treated the King as uncle of the Consul. On landing at Havre the

King walked straight down to the express packet which was lying ready. The Queen went separately, and after making a slight round through the streets of Havre, embarked also. The packet then immediately started and went into Newhaven. General Dumas said that the whole party were unprovided with anything but the clothes they wore, and he was going to the King's banker to provide funds to enable him to come to town, and said that the King begged him to apologise for his not having at once written to Queen Victoria for the interest taken in his safety. It has been explained to General Dumas that arrangements have been made for the King's reception at Claremont. He says that the King and Queen have gone through much personal fatigue and mental anxiety.'

With regard to the new French Government, Lord Palmerston writes to our Ambassador at Paris: 'If the Powers of Europe wished to make war against France there are in the circular [one sent by M. Lamartine] abundant materials wherewith to pick a quarrel with her. If, on the other hand, the Powers of Europe are desirous of maintaining peace, there is to be found in that circular the substance of peace, although clothed in the garb of defiance. It seems to her Majesty's Government that the wisest course which the Governments of Europe can pursue will be to accept the assurances of peace, and of abstinence from aggression, military or political, which that circular contains, and without themselves giving up the obligation of treaties, to refrain from attempting to exact from the Provisional Government any abstract and theoretical acknowledgment of those treaties of which that Government declares itself ready to accept the territorial result as a fact which cannot be altered without the consent of all parties concerned. It may be remarked, however, that there is no doctrine in the Law of Nations more universally acknowledged or more essential as a foundation of international relations, than the principle that a nation does not free itself from its treaty engagements by changing the form of its internal government.'

VII

Palmerston's Foreign Policy
from 1848–1850

THE YEAR 1848 WAS A troubled period in England, and it also marked
an acute crisis in the history of modern Europe. The overthrow of
Louis Philippe accelerated all those social and political forces which have
so largely since that time altered the map of Europe. Lord Palmerston,
sympathising with moderate, constitutional reform, but strongly opposed
to anything like republican government, sought to use the whole influence of England for the twofold purpose of inducing, on the one hand,
the sovereigns of Europe to grant more in the way of reform than any
of them relished, and on the other, of inducing the reformers to be content with less than they desired. In so doing he was but following out the
natural bent of his mind, and the mere statement of the fact is enough to
show why his policy was so bitterly resented by such men as Bright and
Cobden. If it cannot be considered lofty in aim, it was at any rate safe; and
on the whole it achieved quite as large a measure of success as it deserved.

The multitudinous details of this policy, and the bulky volumes of letters
and despatches in which its story is preserved, possess now comparatively
little interest either for the general reader or for the political student. A
much wider space than forty years separates the Europe of 1895 from the
Europe of 1848. It is hardly possible for the young man of to-day to form any
intelligent conception of what Europe was like when Italy was composed
of a multitude of petty sovereignties, when Napoleon III was preparing to
ascend the throne of France, when such questions as Spanish Marriages were
thought to he of prime political importance, and when memoranda such as
the one we are about to quote could be written. It has never appeared in

print before, and is of interest because it gives Palmerston's own version of the policy he pursued at this most critical time with regard to Italy, Austria, Spain, Portugal, and Greece. It is dated July 2, 1848:

'In the autumn of 1847, the Pope, then recently elected, entertained a strong desire to make reforms in the government of his States, a government which had long been known to be more full of practical abuses than any other in Europe. The Pope found himself thwarted by opposing influences from within and from without, and he conveyed to the British Government by several channels, but especially through Lord Shrewsbury and Dr Wiseman, his earnest request that he might receive countenance and support from Great Britain, and that, for this purpose, some agent of the British Government might be sent to Rome; and that if there was any legal impediment to prevent an accredited envoy from being sent to him, he might, nevertheless, have the benefit of the support, assistance, and advice of some person of rank, weight, and, if possible, of diplomatic standing, who might possess the confidence of the British Government, and whose presence at Rome might be a public manifestation of the goodwill of Great Britain. It appeared to the British Government that it would be proper to comply with this application, and it seemed to me that the Earl of Minto, who was then going abroad for a short time with his family, exactly fulfilled the description given by the Pope of the kind of person whom he would wish to have at Rome, and was also peculiarly well qualified to carry out the views of her Majesty's Government. The Earl of Minto was, therefore, sent to Rome. But, in the meantime, fresh complications began to arise in other parts of Italy. The reforms begun, and the further measures announced by the Pope, roused the deeply seated, though long dormant, desires of the people in the other States of Italy for improvements in their respective governments, which, though far better than those of the Papal States, were yet all founded on the arbitrary instead of the constitutional principle. There seemed to be great chance of serious conflict between the sovereigns and their subjects. The sovereigns were averse to making any concessions. The subjects appeared in many places inclined to extort by force concessions unreasonably great. The British Government thought that the mission of the Earl of Minto to Rome might afford an opportunity to Great Britain to exert a useful influence in other parts of Italy; and, accordingly, Lord Minto was instructed to take Turin and Florence on his way to Rome.

'At Turin and Florence Lord Minto was gladly and cordially received, and at these capitals he was able to render important service, both to the sovereign and the subject, by encouraging the Government to grant constitutional institutions, and by exhorting the reform party to accept and to be satisfied with the spontaneous concessions of the sovereign; and I think it may safely be affirmed that the successful exertions of the Earl of Minto at Turin and at Florence were among the principal causes which have saved those capitals from serious convulsion during the last few months. At Rome the same course of policy was pursued, and with the same good results; and, although persons well acquainted with Italy still maintain that the danger of the establishment of republican government in Italy is not yet over, I would fain believe that the reforms and improvements made, and in progress, may succeed in maintaining the monarchical form. From Rome the Earl of Minto went to Naples at the invitation of the King of Naples, and at the request of that sovereign he endeavoured to negotiate a reconciliation between the King and his Sicilian subjects. If the Neapolitan Government had adopted the Earl of Minto's advice, an arrangement would speedily have been made by which the King of Naples would have retained on his own head the Crown of Sicily, but blind prejudice, or ill-founded hopes of assistance from other quarters, prevailed, and the golden opportunity was lost ; the news of the French Revolution reached Palermo, and the Sicilians drew back from the conditions which, in compliance with the wishes of England, they had before been willing to agree to. Still, in deference to the desire expressed by the Earl of Minto on behalf of the British Government, they consented to receive one of the sons of the King of Naples as their sovereign; but again a refusal of the King of Naples frustrated the Earl of Minto's endeavours, and the Sicilians then proceeded to declare the deposal of the Royal Family of Naples, and to look out for some prince of some other Italian house; being impelled partly by their own preference, and partly by the exhortations of British agents to adhere to the monarchical instead of adopting the republican form of government.

'The Earl of Minto having nothing further to detain him in Italy, and being wanted in England, then returned home. I believe that there is nothing in the course of the policy pursued by the British Government in all these Italian affairs that is not honourable to Great Britain, and conducive not only to the advantage of Italy, but also to the general interests of Europe, and to the maintenance of its peace. But there happened in Lombardy, soon after the French Revolution of February, a general rising against the Austrian rule; and so determined and extensive was the insurrection, that the large Austrian garrison of Milan was compelled after a long struggle to evacuate that city.

'The fire of intense dislike to Austrian domination which had so long been kept smothered by overpowering force now burst out into a flame from one end of Italy to the other, and a general crusade was proclaimed to drive the Austrians over the Alps. The King of Sardinia was called on by the people of Lombardy, and urged by his own ministers and subjects, to take part in the war, and to assist in endeavouring to expel the Austrian army. He was told that, if he did not do so, he would run the risk of being dethroned, and that a Republic would probably be declared in his own dominions. 'To these impulses he yielded, urged on at the same time, it cannot be doubted, by his own personal ambition. In the summer of last year, when the King of Sardinia was projecting improvements in his administration, and when the movements of the Austrian force in Lombardy seemed to threaten attack in order to prevent those internal improvements, the British Government made a representation to the Government of Austria for the purpose of dissuading any such attack. Therefore, when it seemed likely that the King of Sardinia would become the assailant against Austria, the British Minister at Turin, without waiting for instructions, which there was no time for him to ask for and to receive, remonstrated strongly upon his own responsibility against the decision which he understood the Government of Turin was about to take, and his conduct in so doing was approved, and fresh instructions to the same effect were sent him. But the representations thus made could not be expected to outweigh the stronger motives which led to the decision, and the Piedmontese army began its march into Lombardy. Remonstrance and argument having failed, the British Government might certainly have gone a step further, and might have intimated an intention of taking part in the war in favour of Austria, and against Piedmont. But such an active interference would have been a grave step, would not have been in unison with public opinion in this country, might probably have been disapproved by Parliament, and would, most likely, have brought France to the assistance of Italy, and perhaps have involved the whole of Europe in war. It only remained, therefore, for us to remain spectators and to watch events.

'Representations similar to those made by Mr Abercromby at Turin were made, by Sir George Hamilton at Florence, and by Lord Napier at Naples, but with a similar result. Popular passions and national antipathies ran far too strong to be controlled by a distant foreign Power; and our diplomatic agents in Italy were instructed to discontinue remonstrances which experience had shown to be unavailing. At last the Austrian Government, justly believing in the desire of our Government to assist Austria if it had the power to do so, sent M. de Hummelauer to London to request the interposition of Great Britain between the Emperor and his revolted subjects in Italy, with a view to negotiate a reconciliation. I declared to M. de Hummelauer that the British Government would gladly undertake the task if Austria would enable them to propose conditions which, in the existing state of things, it was possible to expect that the Italians would agree to. M. de Hummelauer's first proposal was that Lombardy should be erected into an Austrian principality with an archduke at its head, under the Emperor as suzerain, and that the Venetian State should remain as it had been; and that Lombardy should, in consideration of the arrangement, take upon herself a portion of the pecuniary encumbrances of Austria. To this I at once replied that such an arrangement would have been accepted by the people of Lombardy with joyfulness and gratitude in the autumn of last year, but that it was now entirely too late, and would be rejected instantly by the Italians. M. de Hummelauer entirely assented to this opinion, which, he said, was quite his own also; but he had been instructed to make the proposal, and, having done so, he had fulfilled his instructions. He then made a second proposal, which was, that Lombardy should be set free by Austria to dispose of herself as she chose, but taking upon herself a suitable proportion of the pecuniary liabilities of the Austrian Empire; and that the arrangement proposed by the first plan for Lombardy should be applied to the Venetian State. I said this was a plan which I felt I could submit for the consideration of the Cabinet, without of course anticipating what the decision thereupon might be. This proposal was accordingly taken into consideration by the Cabinet; but, whatever may be their wishes that the Austrian Government may remain as strong and undiminished in extent of territory as possible, it did not appear to them that we could offer to negotiate between the parties on such term's, because it did not appear to them that there was any reasonable probability that to such terms the Italians would agree. But I informed M. de Hummelauer that if it should suit the views and opinions of the Austrian Government to open a negotiation with the Italians for relinquishing not only Lombardy, but also such portions of the Venetian territory as might be agreed upon between the parties, Austria receiving pecuniary compensation for her cession, we, believing that an arrangement might be concluded on such a basis, would willingly give our good offices for such a negotiation.

'M. de Hummelauer in reply said that he was not authorised to accept, but, on the other hand, did not think himself authorised to reject, such a scheme of arrangement; that he would immediately return with it to his Government and submit it for their consideration. He, however, intimated to me a half intention on his part to take Paris on his way, and to consult the French Government on the subject, but said he would be guided in that respect by my opinion and I advised him to go straight to his own Government, and not to bring the French Government into the matter until he should be instructed to do so. I have received no reply, but I understand from Lord Ponsonby that the Austrian Government intend to open negotiations with the Government of Lombardy direct, without using the intervention of any other Power.

'In this state of things it occurred to me that some instructions should be given to Mr Abercromby, and I accordingly prepared the Instructions of the 23rd ultimo, in which I stated that if the Venetian State could be retained by Austria, usefully to herself and with the consent of all parties concerned, the British Government would see such an arrangement with pleasure, and that therefore Mr Abercromby was to throw no obstacle in the way of such a settlement; to which, however, I observe that the French Republic has declared itself unwilling to consent. On the other hand, Mr Abercromby was instructed not to encourage the King of Sardinia to abandon the Venetians, because he would not do so unless it suited his own purposes and interests, and if he did so for such motives, and was reproached, as he would be by the Italians, with having abandoned the national cause for his own personal convenience, he would then throw the blame on the British Government, which would thereby lose that influence in Italy, an influence that may continue to be the means of doing good and of preventing evil. Mr Abercromby was, therefore, instructed not to meddle either way with the question about the Venetian State, unless he should be requested to do so by the Venetians themselves. This being the state of the case, there is nothing in the policy we have pursued in regard to Italian affairs that is not perfectly honourable, and which cannot be avowed and justified in the face of the world.

'A comparison has been made between the State of Italy and the State of Sleswig, but there are essential differences between the two as far as Great Britain is concerned. In Sleswig we have been accepted by both parties as mediators, which is not the case in regard to the Italian war, and a Government engaged in mediation may justly urge the contending parties to suspend the progress of the war. In the case of Sleswig, too, there is a treaty guarantee which has been given by the British Crown, which might, if the Danish construction of it were admitted, compel Great Britain to become a party in the war if mediation were unsuccessful. But Mr Abercromby was instructed to represent to the Government of Turin that the arguments by which it justified its advance into Lombardy might be turned against itself if there were an insurrection got up in Savoy, and if the French came to the aid of the insurgents; and I do not recollect at the present moment that anything stronger has been addressed to the Prussian Government in regard to the affair of Sleswig. It has been observed that I pointed out to Chevalier Bunsen in a recent letter that no new territory or state could be added to the German Confederation without the consent of its sovereign, and this has been held to be inconsistent with the proposed incorporation of Lombardy with Piedmont. But the German Confederation is in its form and essence a league of sovereigns, and not a single state, and consequently, until its nature and character is entirely changed, no additional state or territory can be included within the Confederation except by the formal accession of the sovereign of such territory or state to the existing league. There is no *pays de généralité* belonging to the Confederation in its aggregate and corporate capacity, and if the Confederation were to conquer any territory, and wish to include it in the limits of the Confederation, it would be necessary, as matters now stand, that such territory should come under the dominion of some one of the confederate sovereigns, and should by him, by a formal act, be added to the territories included within the Confederation.

'But the case of Lombardy is essentially different. It is that of a province which revolts from one sovereign and transfers its allegiance to another; and the former sovereign is willing to renounce his claim, and to legalise the transfer, in exchange for a pecuniary consideration. In adverting to the question about influence in foreign countries, it has been said that in those countries with regard to which the greatest stress has been laid on that influence, and the greatest exertions have been made to obtain it, the least good has been done by it, as for instance in Spain, Portugal, and Greece.

'But that British influence in Spain was advisedly, though, as I have always ventured to think, most injudiciously, surrendered by the late Government in England, who gave up Spain to France, and instructed Sir H. Bulwer to follow in all respects the lead of the French Ambassador. The Regent, the Duke of Vittoria, who looked to Great Britain for support, because he is a good Spaniard, and knows that England has no object in Spain except the independence and prosperity of Spain, was abandoned to the intrigues of the French Government, and the party who are willing to sacrifice the independence of their country at the shrine of personal interest were placed in power, and have retained it ever since by the same corrupt means and support by which they obtained it. The abandonment of Spain was part of the price paid for that *entente cordiale* which did not prevent the dispute about Tahiti, and which the recent publications in the *Revue Rétrospective* sufficiently show to have been chiefly designed to deceive us and to cajole us, while the King of the French was pursuing his own schemes of family interests and political ambition.

'If British influence had been maintained in Spain as it was in 1841, when Viscount Melbourne's Administration went out, it can hardly be imagined that the two unfortunate Spanish marriages could have been brought about, and if the maintenance of British influence in Spain could have prevented these two lamentable events, it was surely worth while for the British Government to have made some effort for the purpose of maintaining that influence.

'In regard to Portugal, I would observe that it was the influence and action of Great Britain, co-operating as a matter of policy but not as a matter of necessity with France and Spain, that saved the Queen and the King of Portugal from probable dethronement, and if the influence of our Government has not since that time been able to counteract other influences which have led the Queen of Portugal away from a strict and faithful performance of the spirit of her engagements, that influence has at least been one among the causes which have prevented a renewal of disturbance in Portugal.

'In regard to Greece, I think that the state of that country is rather an example of the evil which may arise from the extinction or non-existence of British influence, than of the inutility of creating and maintaining it. No British Government has had any influence in Greece, or, more properly speaking, over the Government at Athens, since the majority of King Otho, or, indeed, it may be said since the end of the regency of the Count Armersperg. But the reason of this circumstance lies in a narrow compass. The British Government, whoever have been the ministers of the Crown, has always advised King Otho first to grant a constitution, and afterwards, when he had been compelled by insurrection to do so, to observe the constitution which he had agreed to. But this advice has always been unpalatable to King Otho, and his aversion to follow it has been backed and supported by the communications which he has till very lately constantly received from the Governments of France, of Austria, of Russia, of Prussia, and of Bavaria.

'When five Powers were advising the King of Greece to follow his own inclinations, and one Power was urging him to do that which he disliked, it was not to be wondered at that the influence of the five should overpower the influence of the one. But the advice and encouragement given by the five have rendered the King hateful to his subjects, have spread insurrection and anarchy throughout the land, and have brought the State to the verge of bankruptcy; while the advice of the one would, if it had been attended to, have bound the subjects by attachment to the sovereign, have established peace and legal order in the country, and would have freed the kingdom from its financial embarrassments.'

An amusing anecdote, communicated to the writer by a friend, illustrates how well Lord Palmerston's name was known in Italy at this time. 'Do you know a story which Edward Lear, the artist, used to tell?—one day, while wandering in the Abruzzi, he entered the gate of a small town, and was stopped by a tipsy gendarme who demanded his passport, and seeing *Palmerston* "writ large" at the bottom of it, hauled him through the streets to the Podestà shouting, "Ho preso Palmerston! Ho preso Palmerston!" ("I have taken Palmerston.")' The smallest Neapolitan official knew the dreaded name.

Lord Palmerston occasionally found it needful to use forcible language in his official correspondence. Challenged on this subject, he thus defended himself in a despatch, October, 1848: 'It is no doubt painful to have to speak of sovereigns in the terms used by Viscount Palmerston in regard to the King of Greece, the late King of Bavaria and the King of the French. But when important public interests are at stake, essential truths ought not to be withheld, and nothing, he is firmly convinced, which he has said of those three sovereigns exceeds the truth. In regard to one of them, he fears that what he said falls short of the truth, and that the defects of the King of Greece lie quite as much in his moral as in his intellectual qualities.'

Such a time of national upheaval could not fail to influence Ireland adversely, and in 1848 some American sympathisers with rebellion in Ireland were arrested, and Lord Palmerston writes as follows regarding the action of the Government to Mr Bancroft, the United States Minister:

'Not only private meetings have been held, but public meetings also for the avowed purpose of encouraging rebel lion in Ireland, and with a view to dismember the British Empire by separating Ireland from the dominion of the British Crown. It is also notorious that these associations and public meetings have been composed not only of Irish emigrants, but also of national-born citizens of the United States, and indeed, among the number of these conspirators against the peace of a country with which the United States are in friendly relations, there is good reason to believe that persons have been found who, for many obvious reasons, it might have been hoped would not have been so engaged. It is perfectly well known that these conspirators in the United States have sent to Ireland, to assist the rebellion which they had intended to organise, money, arms, ammunition, and active agents. Some portions of the arms and ammunition indeed have been seized, and will be confiscated, and some of the agents have been arrested, and must be dealt with according to their deserts. Her Majesty's Government, well knowing the constitutional difficulties of the United States, and convinced that the President has employed to the utmost the very limited means within his power to check and discountenance the proceedings above mentioned, have not pressed the Government of the United States with representations against a state of things which under other circumstances would scarcely have been compatible with the continuance of friendly relations between the two Governments. But then, on the other hand, the Government of the United States must not take it amiss that her Majesty's Government should resort to measures of precaution and of repression in regard to persons, whatever their nationality may be, who in this posture of affairs may come from the United States to this realm; and if there should be any citizens of the United States who have chosen this period of disturbance for visiting Ireland for innocent purposes, they must not be surprised if, like persons whom curiosity may lead into the midst of a battle, they should be involved in the sweep of measures aimed at men of a different description. But her Majesty's Government will always lament if mistakes happen. The utmost alacrity will he evinced by the Irish Government to rectify such errors.'

In March, 1849, we find him thus speaking of the moral influence of England:

'I say, in contradiction to the honourable gentleman, that this country does stand well with the great majority of the foreign Powers—that the character of this country stands high—that the moral influence of England is great—a moral influence that I do not take credit to this Government for having created, but which is founded on the good sense and the wise and enlightened conduct of the British nation. Foreign countries have seen that in the midst of the events which have violently convulsed other countries in Europe, and which have shaken to their foundations ancient institutions, this country has held fast to her ancient landmarks, standing firm in her pride of place:

> Fell not, but stands unshaken, from within,
> Or from without, 'gainst all temptations armed.

That has given confidence to foreign countries in the government and people of this country. When other monarchies were shaken to their very foundations, England stood unhurt, by its evident security giving confidence to other Powers. They have seen that the Government of England is not like that of other countries, struggling for its existence, and occupied in guarding against daily dangers. They have seen that the British Constitution acts in unison with the spirit of the nation, with whose interests it is charged. They know that its advice is worthy of being listened to; and that advice is valued and respected, and is not spurned with contumely, as the honourable member would wish us to suppose.'

During the same session he expressed himself in the House of Commons on June 12, 1849, as against the principle of submitting international disputes to arbitration:

'I confess also that I consider it would be a very dangerous course for this country itself to take, because there is no country which from its political and commercial circumstances, from its maritime interests and from its colonial possessions, excites more envious and jealous feelings in different quarters than England does; and there is no country that would find it more difficult to discover really disinterested and impartial arbiters. There is also no country that would be more likely than England to suffer in its important commercial interest from submitting the case to arbiters, not disinterested, not impartial, and not acting with a due sense of their responsibility.'

In answer to Mr Cobden he said he agreed with him, and with those he represents, in feeling the utmost dislike 'and I may say horror of war in any shape. I will not go further into those commonplace remarks which must be familiar to the mind of every man who has contrasted the calamities of war with the various blessings and advantages which attend upon peace. I cannot conceive that there exists in this country the man who does not attach the utmost value to the blessings of peace, and who would not make the greatest sacrifices to save his country from the calamities attendant upon war. It will be useful for England and for Europe at large that every man should know that in this assembly, and among the vast masses of men of whom we are the representatives, there is a sincere and honest disposition to maintain peace. But that which I wish to guard against—the impression that I wish should not be entertained anywhere, either in this country or out of it—is, that while there is in England a fervent love of peace, an anxious and steady desire to maintain it, there should not exist the impression that the manly spirit of Englishmen is dead; that England is not ready, as she is ever, to repel aggression and resent injury; and that she never will be found acting aggressively against any other Power. It would be most dangerous indeed to the interests of peace that a contrary opinion should prevail. I can conceive nothing that would bring more into jeopardy our peaceful relations than that an idea should prevail among foreign nations that we are so attached to peace that we dare not make war, and that therefore any aggression or any injury may be safely ventured against English subjects, because England has such a rooted aversion to war that she will not repel it.'

And soon after he spoke again to the same effect: 'I cannot condemn that provident provision of things which cannot be created at a moment's notice, and which would be necessary if we were called on to defend ourselves from foreign aggression—and the chance of which, if known to foreign countries, would form an incitement and temptation to commit wrong against this country. I think that a Government acts wisely and prudently when they gradually, and without overstraining the burden on the country, lay up a store of those things which may be wanted on the first outbreak of a war, if it should unfortunately occur, and which must be provided for beforehand, while they abstain from useless augmentations of men, which can be raised when the emergency arises, and in a short period would be just as effective as if they had been longer in military training.'

In 1849 Hungary attempted to throw off the Austrian yoke, and but for the assistance given to the latter by Russia would in all probability have succeeded. The insurrection was repressed with great violence, and the most inhuman cruelties were inflicted upon the insurgents. Kossuth and other Hungarians took refuge in Turkey, and when Austria and Russia jointly demanded their surrender, Palmerston supported the Sultan in his refusal to comply with their demand. Nearly two years, however, elapsed before they were released by the Sultan and enabled to come to England. It was in connection with these negotiations that Palmerston applied to his work an image derived from the prize-fighter's arena, a spot not unfamiliar to the Foreign Minister, if common report may be relied upon. He said that 'during the struggle a good deal of judicious bottle-holding was obliged to be brought into play.' This was at once seized upon by *Punch* and used with great effect.

In speaking on behalf of Austria at this time he gave at some length his views on the part that England should play in maintaining that most shadowy and most costly of diplomatic entities 'the balance of power.' 'There are higher and larger considerations which ought to render the maintenance of the Austrian Empire an object of solicitude to every English statesman. Austria is a most important element in the balance of European power. Austria stands in the centre of Europe, a barrier against encroachments on the one side and against invasion on the other. The political independence and liberties of Europe are bound up, in my opinion, with the maintenance and integrity of Austria as a great European Power; and, therefore, anything which tends by direct or even remote contingency to weaken and cripple Austria, but still more to reduce her from her position of a first-rate Power to that of a secondary State, must be a great calamity to Europe, and one which every Englishman ought to deprecate and endeavour to prevent. It is perfectly true, as has been stated, that for a long course of time Austria has not been a favourite with the Liberal party in Europe. Austria, by the course of policy which she has pursued, has, in the opinion of a great part of the Continent, been identified with obstruction to progress. That circumstance unfortunately has made her proportionately a favourite in the eyes of some, and when we hear such declarations in favour of Austria, I would warn the Austrian Government not to trust too much to those protestations. It is not as the ancient ally of England during war—it is not as the means of resistance in the centre of Europe to any general disturbance of the balance of power—it is as the former symbol of resistance to improvement—political and social—it is in that capacity that Austria has won the affections of some men in the conduct of public affairs. I shall not be expected to pass judgment between the Austrian Government and the Hungarian nation. I say the Hungarian nation, because I firmly believe that in this war between Austria and Hungary there is enlisted on the side of Hungary the hearts and souls of the whole people of that country. I believe that the other races distinct from the Magyars have forgotten the former feuds that existed between them and the Magyar population, and that the greater portion of the people have engaged in what they consider a great national contest. It is true that Hungary for centuries past has been a State which, though united with Austria by the link of the Crown, has nevertheless been separated and distinct from Austria by its own complete constitution. That constitution has many defects, but some were remedied not long ago, and it is not the only ancient constitution on the Continent which was susceptible of improvement. There were means probably within the force and resources of the constitution itself to reform it, and it might have been hoped that these improvements would have been carried into effect. I take the question which is now to be fought out on the plains of Hungary to be this: whether Hungary shall continue to maintain its separate nationality as a distinct kingdom, and with a constitution of its own; or whether it is to be incorporated more or less in the aggregate constitution that is to be given to the Austrian Empire. It is a most painful sight to see such forces as are now arrayed against Hungary proceeding to a war fraught with such tremendous consequences on a question that might have been settled peaceably. It is of the utmost importance to Europe that Austria shall remain great and powerful; but it is impossible to disguise from ourselves that, if the war is to be fought out, Austria must thereby be weakened, because if the Hungarians should be successful, and their success should end in the entire separation of Austria from Hungary, it will be impossible not to see that this would be such a dismemberment of the Austrian Empire as will prevent Austria from continuing to occupy the great position she has hitherto held among European Powers; if, on the other hand, the war being fought out to the uttermost, Hungary should be completely crushed by superior forces, Austria, in that battle, will have crushed her own right arm. Every field that is laid waste is an Austrian resource destroyed, every man that perishes on the field among the Hungarian ranks is an Austrian soldier deducted from the defensive forces of the Empire. It is devoutly to be wished that this great contest may be brought to a termination by some amicable treaty between the contending parties, which shall on the one hand satisfy the national feelings of the Hungarians, and yet not leave to Austria another and a larger Poland within her borders. We have been accused of meddling with matters that do not concern us, and of affronting nations and governments by giving an opinion as to what was likely to happen; but the result has proved that, if our opinions had been acted upon, great calamities would have been avoided. These very Governments used to say, "The man we hate, the man we have to fear, is the Moderate Reformer. We care not for your violent Radical, who proposes such violent extremes that nobody is likely to join with him; the enemy we are most afraid of is the Moderate Reformer, because he is such a plausible man, that it is difficult to persuade people that his counsels would lead to extreme consequences; therefore let us keep off of all men the Moderate Reformer, and let us prevent the first step of improvement, because that improvement might lead to extremities and innovation." These Governments, these Powers of Europe, have at last learned the truth of the opinion expressed by Canning, that those who have checked improvement because it is innovation, will one day or other be compelled to accept innovation when it has ceased to be improvement.

'I say then that it is our duty not to remain passive spectators of events that in their immediate consequences affect other countries, but which in their remote and certain consequences are sure to come back with disastrous effect upon ourselves; that, so far as the courtesies of international intercourse may permit us to do, it is our duty, especially when our opinion is asked, as it has been on many occasions on which we have been blamed for giving it, to state our opinions, founded on the experience of this country, an experience that might have been, and ought to have been, an example to less fortunate countries. At the same time I am quite ready to admit that interference ought not to be carried to the extent of endangering our relations with other countries. There are cases, like that of Austria and Hungary, of one Power having in the exercise of its own sovereign rights invited the assistance of another Power; and however we may lament that circumstance, however we may be apprehensive that there from consequences of great danger and evil may flow, still we are not entitled to interfere in any manner that will commit this country to embark in these hostilities. All we can justly do is to take advantage of any opportunities that may present themselves in which the counsels of friendship and peace may be offered to the contending parties. We have on several occasions that have happened of late in Europe been invited to "intermeddle" as it is called in the affairs of other countries, although it has been said of this country that it stands so low in public opinion in Europe that we are treated with contempt both by governments and nations. Certainly the way in which that want of respect has been shown is singular, when from the north to the south, in cases of difficulty not only between nations, but internally between governments and their own subjects, we have been asked and invited to interpose our friendly mediation in their affairs. We have on those occasions done our best to accomplish the object which we were called upon to fulfil. We have heard a great deal of "sham mediation" in the contest between Germany and Denmark, but that sham mediation has ended in a real preliminary treaty, and I hope that will soon be followed by permanent pacification. Sir, to suppose that any government of England can wish to excite revolutionary movements in any part of the world—to suppose that any government of England can have any other wish or desire than to confirm and maintain peace between nations, and tranquillity and harmony between governments and subjects—shows a degree of ignorance and folly which I never supposed any public man could be guilty of—which may do very well for a newspaper article, but which, it astonishes me to find, is made the subject of a speech in Parliament.

'We have been told that Austria is our ancient ally. We have had the terms "ally" and "allies" rung in our ears by those who either must be ignorant of the slipslop expression they are using, or who, through what I must admit to have been its general acceptation, forget that they were using a totally unmeaning term. Why, what is an ally? An ally is a Power allied by treaty engagements in carrying on some active operations, political or otherwise. But to call a country an ally merely because it is in a state of friendship with you is to use an expression that has no meaning whatever, because it is applicable to every other Power in the world with whom you may happen not to be in a state of war. But Austria has been our ally. We have been allied with Austria in most important European transactions; and the remembrance of the alliance ought undoubtedly to create in the breast of every Englishman who has a recollection of the history of his country feelings of respect towards a Power with whom we have been in such alliance.'

At the same time Lord Palmerston never disguised his abhorrence of the methods employed by Austria in suppressing the Hungarian revolt. 'The Austrians,' he says in a letter dated September 9, 1849, 'are really the greatest brutes that ever called themselves by the undeserved name of civilised men.' In 1850 General Haynau, a man most notorious for his cruelty, and said to have inflicted floggings upon women, came to London, and visited the brewery of Messrs. Barclay and Perkins. There he was assailed by the draymen, and finally rescued by the police. In reply to the Austrian demand for satisfaction, Lord Palmerston very clearly and coolly stated the merits of the case: 'The people of this country are remarkable for their hospitable reception of foreigners, and for their forgetfulness of past animosities. Napoleon Buonaparte, the greatest enemy that England ever had, was treated while at Plymouth with respect, and with commiseration while at St. Helena. Marshal Soult, who had fought in many battles against the English, was received with generous acclamation when he came here as special ambassador. The King of the French, M. Guizot, and Prince Metternich, though all of them great antagonists of English policy and English interests, were treated in this country with courtesy and kindness. But General Haynau was looked upon as a great moral criminal; and the feeling in regard to him was of the same nature as that which was manifested towards the Mannings, with this only difference, that General Haynau's bad deeds were committed upon a far larger scale, and upon a far larger number of victims. The feelings of just and honourable indignation have not been confined to England.'

Lord Palmerston's somewhat high-handed policy met with constant opposition in the House of Commons, although it was received with warm approval by the majority of the members. The Whig Ministry of 1850, like the Liberal administrations of later days, had a solid Tory majority against them in the House of Lords, and on June 17, 1850, Lord Stanley, by a majority of thirty-seven, carried a resolution affirming 'that various claims against the Greek Government, doubtful in point of justice or exaggerated in amount, have been enforced by coercive measures directed against the commerce and people of Greece, and calculated to endanger the continuance of our friendly relations with other Powers.' In reply to this, on June 24, Mr Roebuck moved in the House of Commons, 'that the principles on which the foreign policy of her Majesty's Government has been regulated have been such as were calculated to maintain the honour and dignity of this country, and in times of unexampled difficulty to preserve peace between England and the various nations of the world.' A four-nights' debate ensued, and on the second Lord Palmerston delivered the famous speech which occupied nearly five hours, and in which he gave an elaborate vindication of his whole foreign policy. The house of Don Pacifico, a Jew, a native of Gibraltar, had been sacked in open day in Athens by a Greek mob, headed by the sons of the Greek Minister of War. All demands for redress in his case and many others being treated with contempt, Lord Palmerston finally sent the fleet to the Piraeus and seized certain vessels there. This action, and the subsequent international complications, gave rise to the debate. Lord Palmerston's speech marks an era in his career. It is now of moment chiefly for two passages, which we quote. In the first, by a clever use of illustration, he sketches himself:

'However, sir, the right hon. baronet (Sir J. Graham) says that these affairs of Spain were of long duration, and produced disastrous consequences, because they were followed by events of the greatest importance as regards another country, namely, France. He says that out of those Spanish quarrels and Spanish marriages there arose differences between England and France which led to no slighter catastrophe than the overthrow of the French monarchy. This is another instance of the fondness for narrowing down a great and national question to the smallness of personal difference. It was my dislike to M. Guizot, forsooth, arising out of these Spanish marriages, which overthrew his Administration, and with it the throne of France! Why, sir, what will the French nation say when they hear this? They are a high-minded and high-spirited nation, full of a sense of their own dignity and honour. What will they say when they hear it stated that it was in the power of a British Minister to overthrow their Government and their monarchy? (Much cheering.) Why, sir, it is a calumny on the French nation to suppose that the personal hatred of any foreigner to their Minister could have this effect. They are a brave, a generous, and a noble-minded people; and if they had thought that a foreign conspiracy had been formed against one of their Ministers—(tremendous and prolonged cheering, which prevented the noble Viscount from concluding the sentence) —I say, that if the French people had thought that a knot of foreign conspirators were caballing against one of their Ministers, and caballing for no other reason than that he upheld, as he conceived, the dignity and interests of his own country, and if they had thought that such a knot of foreign conspirators had coadjutors in their own land, why, I say that the French people, that brave, noble, and spirited nation, would have scorned the intrigues of such a cabal, and would have clung the closer to, and have supported the more, the man against whom such a plot had been made.'

In the second we have the most effective peroration Lord Palmerston ever delivered:

'I believe I have now gone through all the heads of the charges which have been brought against me in this debate. I think I have shown that the foreign policy of the Government in all the transactions with respect to which its conduct has been impugned, has throughout been guided by those principles which, according to the resolution of the honourable and learned gentleman, ought to regulate the conduct of the Government of England in the management of our foreign affairs. I believe that the principles on which we have acted are those which are held by the great mass of the people of this country. I am convinced these principles are calculated, so far as the influence of England may properly be exercised with respect to the destinies of other countries, to conduce to the maintenance of peace, to the advancement of civilisation, to the welfare and happiness of mankind.

'I do not complain of the conduct of those who have made these matters the means of attack upon her Majesty's Ministers. The government of a great country like this is, undoubtedly, an object of fair and legitimate ambition to men of all shades of opinion. It is a noble thing to be allowed to guide the policy and to influence the destiny of such a country; and if ever it was an object of honourable ambition, more than ever must it be so at the moment at which I am speaking. For while we have seen, as stated by the right honourable baronet, the political earthquake rocking Europe from side to side—while we have seen thrones shaken, shattered, levelled, institutions overthrown and destroyed—while in almost every country of Europe the conflict of civil war has deluged the land with blood, from the Atlantic to the Black Sea, from the Baltic to the Mediterranean, this country has presented a spectacle honourable to the people of England and worthy of the admiration of mankind.

'We have shown that liberty is compatible with order; that individual freedom is reconcilable with obedience to the law. We have shown the example of a nation in which every class of society accepts with cheerfulness the lot which Providence has assigned to it, while at the same time every individual of each class is constantly striving to raise himself in the social scale—not by injustice and wrong, not by violence and illegality, but by persevering good conduct, and by the steady and energetic exertion of the moral and intellectual faculties with which his Creator has endowed him. To govern such a people as this is indeed an object worthy of the ambition of the noblest man who lives in the land, and, therefore, I find no fault with those who may think any opportunity a fair one for endeavouring to place themselves in so distinguished and honourable a position but I contend that we have not in our foreign policy done anything to forfeit the confidence of the country. We may not, perhaps, in this matter or in that have acted precisely up to the opinions of one person or of another; and hard indeed it is, as we all know by our individual and private experience, to find any number of men agreeing entirely in any matter on which they may not be equally possessed of the details of the facts, circumstances, reasons, and conditions which led to action. But, making allowance for those differences of opinion which may fairly and honourably arise among those who concur in general views, I maintain that the principles which can be traced through all our foreign transactions, as the guiding rule and directing spirit of our proceedings, are such as deserve approbation.

'I therefore fearlessly challenge the verdict which this House, as representing a political, a commercial, a constitutional country, is to give on the question now brought before it—whether the principles on which the foreign policy of her Majesty's Government has been conducted, and the sense of duty which has led us to think ourselves bound to afford protection to our fellow-subjects abroad, are proper and fitting guides for those who are charged with the government of England; and whether, as the Roman in days of old held himself free from indignity when he could say, *Civis Romanus sum,* so also a British subject, in whatever land he may be, shall feel confident that the watchful eye and the strong arm of England will protect him against injustice and wrong.'

Although opposed by Sir Robert Peel and Mr Disraeli, and by Mr Gladstone in one of the ablest speeches that great orator ever delivered, *Civis Romanus sum* triumphed and Lord Palmerston secured a majority of fifty-six, and made a long stride towards that legitimate goal of a statesman's ambition: the Premiership of England.

VIII

The Summary Dismissal from the Foreign Office

IN THE YEAR 1851 THE dispute occurred between Lord Russell and Lord Palmerston, which led to the Foreign Office being given to Lord Granville. It had always been Lord Palmerston's custom in his negotiations not only to use the weapons of the arguments of official despatches, but also to employ very largely private correspondence, and semi-official or personal representation of the case he desired to enforce. He used to say that such a method of procedure was often necessary to the smooth working of affairs. 'You may as from yourself,' he would write to an ambassador, 'say to the King, or to the minister, that it will be to his interest to act in such and such a way.' Of these communications to British representatives abroad there was, of course, no trace left in any official correspondence. The official despatch sent with the concurrence of the Cabinet would perhaps follow the same general argument or even use the same phrases; but often the private letter, or the inculcation of a particular tone on our plenipotentiary in dealing with the ministers of a foreign Power, was not in strict accordance with what would appear publicly in the Blue Book submitted to Parliament. It was essential, Lord Palmerston said, that a Foreign Minister should be allowed to work in this way.

But some of Lord Palmerston's colleagues were very jealous of such exercise of influence. The reasons given against anything being sent except the letters known to the Cabinet were briefly that 'a man must either write, when Foreign Secretary, letters for which in that capacity he is prepared to be publicly answerable, or if he writes as a private person he must not ask the British Minister, if the British Minister at a foreign capital be his correspondent, to press the views given in a private letter, because for such his colleagues at home *cannot* be answerable, and they do not even know the purport of such practically secret communications.' 'Speak either as Foreign Secretary or not at all in such matters,' was the language used by men distrustful of Lord Palmerston's tendencies. 'No; public matters can be softened and disputes prevented by my private letters,' said Lord Palmerston in effect, and he continued to act on the idea to the last.

He himself would come down sharply enough on a subordinate member of the Government if things were done without his knowledge in even such comparatively unimportant matters as the arrangements in the public parks. 'I saw a lot of men enclosing plots of grass, and commencing plantations,' he wrote to the head of the Board of Works on one occasion; 'the grass is made for the public to walk upon, and I will not, as head of the Government, be responsible for the limitation you are putting on their enjoyment of the grass.' But he never found fault when Prime Minister with any letters a colleague may have written to prevent misunderstandings abroad; and always considered that private letters, properly used, and so-called unofficial talk and representations, often took away the necessity of the writing of any despatch on the point on which friction and misunderstanding had arisen.

From this habit it may have happened that he was apt to take a too independent line, and do things on his own responsibility which should only have been done with the consent of his colleagues. It can readily be imagined that a habit of this kind might grow, and that it was tolerably certain to lead to friction. The Queen and the Prince Consort paid great attention to foreign affairs, and they were not likely to approve of the total disregard which sometimes followed suggestions made by them in the drafts of despatches submitted to them. Remonstrances from Lord John Russell and a memorandum from the Queen herself had no perceptible effect. Moreover, there can be no reasonable doubt that he acted with precipitation when his old acquaintance, Louis Napoleon, effected the *coup d'Etat* in 1851. Comparisons were used by Lord Palmerston in his communications with the new Government at Paris which would not have been sanctioned if they had been previously read to the Cabinet. I give his own account of his letter, and of the motives that led to its being written:

'To say that I expressed entire approbation of what the President had done is giving a high colour to anything I may have said ... The opinion I entertain of this grave and important matter is, that so decided an antagonism had grown up between the President and the Assembly, that it was to be foreseen that they could not long co-exist, and that each was planning the overthrow of the other; either meaning aggression, or believing that their cause was only self-defence; and there are circumstances which seem to countenance the supposition that the Assembly intended in the course of that very week to have struck a blow at the President, and to have deprived him of his position. Now, as between the President and the Assembly, it seems to me that the interests of France, and through them the interests of the rest of Europe, were better consulted by the prevalence of the President than they would have been by the prevalence of the Assembly, and the great rise which has taken place in the French funds, from 91 to 102, together with the sudden spring which has been made by commerce in general, seem to show that the French people in general are of the same opinion, and that what has happened has inspired the nation with a feeling of confidence which they had not before. Indeed, to account for this, we have only to look at what each of the two parties offered to France as the result of their victory over the other party.

'The President had to offer unity of authority and purpose, and the support of the whole army against the anarchists for the maintenance of order. The Assembly had to offer immediate division among themselves, a division in the army, and in all probability civil war, during which the anarchists would have had immense opportunities and facilities for carrying their desolating schemes into execution. If the Assembly had had any acceptable ruler to propose to the nation instead of Louis Napoleon, they might with their opinions and preferences have been acting as true patriots by overthrowing the President. But there were scarcely more than three alternatives which they could have proposed. First, Henry V, who represents the principle of legitimacy, and who has a devoted and considerable party in France; but that party is still a minority of the nation, and the minority cannot govern the majority. Secondly, they might have proposed the Count de Paris, but he is only about twelve years old, and a six years' minority with a regency, and with Thiers as a Prime Minister, was not a proposal which a nation in a state in which the French are was at all likely to accept. Thirdly, they might have offered the Prince de Joinville as a President, or three of the generals as a commission of government but neither of these arrangements would have been acceptable to the whole nation. The success, then, of the Assembly would in all human probability have been civil war, while the success of the President promised the return of order.

'This bitter antagonism between the President and the Assembly was partly the consequence of the arrangement of 1848, and partly the result of faults on both sides, but chiefly on the side of the Assembly. It may safely be affirmed that a long duration of a centralised, as contra-distinguished from a federal, republic in a great country like France, with a large standing army, and the seat of government not in an unimportant place like Washington, but in a great capital, which exercises almost paramount influence over the whole country, is a political impossibility, let the arrangement of such a republic be ever so well and so wisely constituted. But the arrangements of 1848 greatly increased that general impossibility, and indeed the work of MM. Marrast and Tocqueville would more properly be called a dissolution than a constitution, for they brought the political organisation of France to the very brink of anarchy. I need only mention among other defects that there were two great powers, each deriving its existence from the same source, almost sure to disagree, with no umpire to decide between them, and neither able by any legal way to get rid of the other; not to dwell upon that, the question in regard to which the rupture took place was sure to bring about sooner or later collision, and probably violence. The constitution contained a regulation that the same person should not be twice running elected as President; that is, the French nation should not, after the first term was over, be allowed to choose the person they might prefer and think fittest to be at the head of their government. Now there seemed every reason to expect that the vast majority of the nation would re-elect Louis Napoleon, and the great majority of the *Conseils-Généraux* petitioned that the constitution might be altered, meaning especially in this respect. But another regulation of 1848 interfered. A certain proportion of the Assembly was required to give validity to a resolution that the constitution should be revised, and that majority the Assembly did not give.

'It had been generally expected that the actual conflict would be put off till May next year, but the measures of both parties brought it on sooner. The proposal of the Parliament to restore universal suffrage was evidently intended for the purpose of securing for him such an overwhelming number of votes that the Assembly could not have set his election aside. The Assembly tried to parry this by various schemes either projected or actually put forward. One plan was a law attaching punishment to any elector who might vote for an ineligible candidate, but this, I believe, was not actually brought forward. Another was what was called the Question proposal, which went to place a portion of the army under the orders of the Assembly. This indeed was negatived, but it showed what its proposers intended. Then came the proposal to declare it high treason in an existing President to take any step to procure his re-election, a law which, if it had passed, would have obviously placed the President at the mercy of the Assembly unless he could rely upon a sufficient portion of the army to fight against that part of it which might go over to the Assembly. It is said, with what truth I cannot tell, that it was the intention of the leaders of the majority of the Assembly, if that law had been carried, immediately to have arrested within the walls and on the spot such of the Ministers as were members, among whom was the Minister of War, and to have also endeavoured to have sent the President to Vincennes ... It seems to me, then, that it is fair to suppose that Louis Napoleon may have acted from mixed motives. There is no doubt that he was impelled by ambition, and by a rooted belief, which he was well known to have entertained from a very early age, that he was destined to govern France. But he may also have felt that in the present deplorable state of society in France he was much more capable of promoting the interests of his country than his antagonists were, and a man even with less personal ambition might in his situation have thought *salus Reipublicae suprema lex*. His justification will very much depend upon the degree of proof which he may be able to adduce, that he was acting at the moment in self-defence, and was only anticipating an impending blow.'

The obvious rejoinder to this memorandum—that the point in dispute was not his judgment or the reasons upon which it was based, but the fact that he had given an opinion without consulting the Cabinet and the Queen—was at once made. Lord Palmerston replied that if a Foreign Minister were never to converse with an Ambassador unless he previously consulted his Cabinet there would be an end to that friendly intercourse which acted so often as oil to the diplomatic machine. Lord John Russell's rejoinder to this was a curt letter to the effect that he had asked her Majesty to appoint a successor to Lord Palmerston.

A letter from Lord Grey on Palmerston's removal shows that, although in 1845 he had refused to join a Ministry in which Palmerston was to be

Foreign Minister, and was alleged by Mr Ellice to have said that he never wished to see Lord Palmerston at the Foreign Office, his feelings had undergone a marked change. In any case his language is most cordial in 1851:

'*December* 23, 1851.—My dear Palmerston, I cannot forbear writing to you to express the great concern with which I learnt at the Cabinet yesterday that you are to retire from the Government. I had not even the suspicion of the probability of such an occurrence until I was informed by Lord Lansdowne at the Grange on Sunday of the correspondence which had taken place between yourself and Lord John, and that the Cabinet which had been summoned had reference to it. Even then I did not suppose that the matter was so serious as I found it to be when I heard the correspondence read in the Cabinet, or that the difference was one which would not be settled without your retirement. Though I have not hesitated on one or two occasions to express openly in the Cabinet my regret at some steps you have taken, I have had too many opportunities of admiring the energy and ability with which you have conducted your important department, and of knowing how much you have contributed to maintain the administration; and I have also more than once had too much reason to feel personally indebted to you for your support not to be much grieved at what has happened. I should not perhaps have written you this letter, were it not for what occurred in December 1845, but, having thought it necessary in the circumstances in which we then were placed to object to your being appointed to the Foreign Office, it seemed to me only right, after having served with you five years and a half; during which time we have always been on friendly terms, and I hope I have given you no reason to doubt my having acted fairly by you as a colleague, that I should now express to you the very great regret I sincerely feel for what has occurred. Believe me yours very faithfully, GREY.'

To this letter Lord Palmerston replied:

'My dear Grey,—I am very much obliged to you for your kind and friendly letter, and I can with great pleasure and truth confirm what you say, that during the five years and a half that we have been acting together as members of the same Cabinet the previous difference of December 1845 has never had any influence on our relations, official or private, and that our intercourse has been as friendly as if that incident had never taken place. What I am now saying to you I have often said to others. Yours sincerely, PALMERSTON.'

The 'fall' of the powerful Foreign Minister caused a great sensation both in Great Britain and on the Continent. An extract from the *Examiner* of that date summarises much public opinion:

'Certain it is that his best friends and admirers have often wished that the manner of his correspondence had been as clear of objection as the matter and subject. Few men acceding to power have been greeted with so general an expression of admiration as has followed Lord Palmerston's retirement. Few rising suns have been more gloriously painted than his setting sun.'

In closing this chapter we may refer to an amusing instance of the way in which Lord Palmerston was determined to let his views be known 'in the proper quarter,' no matter what others of his Government at home might think of the action which excited either his approval or his condemnation. The incident occurred at Macao. The sun was high and the weather beautiful at that port one summer day. The town was crowded with natives and 'foreign devils,' for a *festa* was to be honoured by a religious procession through the streets, and a High Mass and impressive music and ceremonies were to be seen and heard in the cathedral. The bells were jingling and intoning their confused calls from every steeple, and below the belfries the buildings of the town, which covered the slope of the land down to the water's edge, shadowed streets filled with holiday crowds. At anchor in the port lay one of her Britannic Majesty's frigates, commanded by Captain Keppel, the same gallant officer who is now Sir Harry, Admiral of the Fleet. Soon word was brought to Captain Keppel in his ship that during the progress of the procession, which had been slowly making its way over the steep roadways to the church above, accompanied by the priests with the holy wafer and the officials of the place, including the Governor, there had happened an unfortunate occurrence.

A young English clergyman from Shanghai or Canton, or a mere passenger in some passing steamer, had happened to be in the street when the array of priests, acolytes, prelates, and officials, all decked out in sumptuous canonicals or in uniforms, had walked past, and had failed to remove his hat and to bow bareheaded as the sacred emblems went by. He had been arrested, and it was feared he had been put into the common gaol. Keppel had the same liking that Palmerston had of expressing his opinion when any act derogatory to the dignity of a 'Britisher' had been perpetrated by a foreigner. So, after stamping once or twice up and down his deck, he ordered one of his officers to go forthwith and demand of the Governor an explanation of their proceeding of the arrest of the English clergyman, and to insinuate that he must be at once released. The lieutenant went and returned with one of the Governor's staff, who with much gesticulation assured Keppel that what had been done could not be undone. The gallant captain said that he could not parley with one of the Governor's officers, for he, the gallant captain, was her Majesty's representative while in command of her Majesty's war vessel at that port, and that he must ask that the Governor himself should say anything there was to be said.

So the subordinate returned, and his Excellency the Governor himself was soon seen coming off from shore, and was rowed alongside, looking very sulky, very pompous, but in very fine uniform, his flag floating at a little flagstaff in the stern of his boat, his men in tolerably good-looking white dresses, and the whole party heated and embarrassed. As soon as the deck of the British frigate was reached and bows had been exchanged, the captain, who possessed, as all the service knows, a pluck in a quantity contrary to the number of his own inches, looked up at the tall and slim foreign functionary, and asked, was it true he had imprisoned one of her Majesty's subjects? The olive countenance, with its dark moustache, much agitated, looked down on the robust countenance and bushy eyebrows of the British commander, and explained with much energy that it was most unfortunate that disrespect had been shown not only to the Host but to himself, the Governor, by the young Englishman who had contravened the law, and that what had been done could not be helped, and much more to the same purpose. Keppel's brows did not relax, as the Governor may have expected they would, after such an exercise of his eloquence. On the contrary, they made the expression of the blue eyes much more trenchant, and the words came forth as an order, 'That doesn't make the matter a bit better—the man must be at once set at liberty.' Then did every one of the foreign party shrug his shoulders, as their chief gave the example, and voluminous vociferations declared the liberation impossible. Keppel was quite quiet, and when a pause came in the ejaculations he took out his watch and said, 'Now, sir, you will go ashore, and if in twenty minutes after you land the man is not liberated, I land and I liberate him myself.' There was no disobeying the first order, but the second the Governor again repeated to be impossible of fulfilment. The official's boat reached the town. Twenty minutes passed. There was no sign. Keppel's marines and blue-jackets were ready on his deck. They filled the boats, which rowed ashore bristling with bayonets.

There was no opposition to their landing. The local forces were evidently quite unprepared to offer any. The men were formed on the quays, a guard left with the boats, and with Keppel at the head of the little column, an advance was instantly made through the streets to the gaol. There was the greatest excitement among the people; cries and crowding at every corner and along the narrow thoroughfares. Presently the prison came into sight across a piazza. Here all was consternation and fear. The gaoler's daughter was hurried down the stairs with the keys, and handed them out of a window to the nearest bluejacket, and her hurry and fright were so great that as she leant out to hand the keys she overbalanced herself; and fell into his arms, keys and all. Then the door was unlocked and the young English aspirant for martyrdom released, none the worse, and marched down to the shore, and placed for safety on board. Again there was no incident, but noise and excitement among the outraged Governor's subjects. But the affair of course got wind at home, and it was equally of course that some of our friends in the House of Commons, who cannot see a good joke, made the cause of the Governor their own, and the Admiralty of that day being not all composed of men like Keppel, and perhaps being rather glad—some of them—to have a fling at him as being of a different stamp to themselves, sent to him a formal letter of reprimand for the action he had taken. Lord Palmerston knew perfectly well of this letter of the Admiralty, and he was himself at the time the Foreign Minister of Britain. He took good care that by the same mail that took the Admiralty's reprimand, Keppel should receive a formal letter from himself thanking Keppel for the manner in which he had acted and supported the consideration due to one of her Majesty's subjects in a foreign town. Lord Palmerston had the pleasure years afterwards of recommending the gallant officer for a good post on shore.

A letter written to his brother William in January, 1850, throws some light upon those peculiarities in Lord Palmerston's mode of conducting the business of his office which brought him into conflict with the Court and his leader:

'Our shooting has been but indifferent, owing to a bad breeding season, following upon two previous years of the same kind, together with a good poaching season at Romsey. But I have been able to get out three or four times with the hounds, which always does me more good than anything else. Our session will begin the last day of the month. We shall probably have a sharp fire from the Protectionists at starting, but they can make no permanent or material impression either on the House or the country, and they are wholly unable to form a Government even if the offer to do so could be made to them. How do you get on with your demands on the Neapolitan Government for compensation for the two merchants for losses during the civil war? We have given Admiral Parker instructions to go to Athens when he leaves the seas of the Levant, and to back up Wyse in enforcing certain demands which have been long pending before the Greek Government for compensation for British subjects for various wrongs at different times done to them. Of course you will say nothing about this till you hear that it has been done; but when the account of Parker's visit to Athens reaches Naples, you may as well confidentially, and not in pursuance of instructions, but as the result of your own good wishes to avert disagreeable events from Naples, suggest to the Neapolitan Minister the possibility that Parker might receive orders to pay a similar visit to Naples for a like purpose; and that it might be as well for the Neapolitan Government to prevent this by doing with a good grace that which in such a case they might find it best policy to do, although with a bad grace and with some derogation to the dignity of the King; at all events, I wish you would write me an official despatch reporting what you have done in consequence of the instructions which I sent you some months ago upon these matters.'

This letter illustrates a method often pursued by Lord Palmerston himself, and often inculcated on his subordinates, the method of speaking confidentially and unofficially although the speaker may be an official. Strait doctrinal officialism would say, 'You must, if in office, speak only in your public capacity; if you say more or less in private than you are warranted to say in public you betray in one way or the other the trust reposed in you.' But Lord Palmerston always maintained that much good might be done by a Minister speaking sometimes as from himself, and not publicly as though the mouthpiece of his Government. He used to say it smoothed difficulties and poured oil into the wheels of the machinery of diplomacy to do so, but experience in his case no less than others proved that whether it helped diplomacy or no, it certainly produced friction with his colleagues.

Two or three extracts from the 'Greville Memoirs' illustrate some other peculiarities in Palmerston's methods:

'Much talk with Beauvale, particularly about Palmerston; he told me an anecdote of him which shows the man and how difficult he is to manage. During the Spanish discussions Beauvale was at Windsor, and one day when the Prizi was in his room the draft of a despatch from Palmerston arrived to Lord John Russell, which he wanted to show to the Prince, and afterwards to submit to the Queen for her sanction … There was a paragraph in it saying the succession of the Duchesse de Montpensier's children would be inadmissible by the constitutional law of Spain. Lord John said he thought this ought to be expunged …' [The Prince, Beauvale, and the Queen concurred. The paragraph was struck out.] The despatch 'was returned so altered to Palmerston; but when the despatch was published, it was found that Palmerston had reinserted the paragraph, and so it stood. What more may have passed I know not, but it is clear that they all *stood* it, as they always will.'

Again, in 1849, Greville writes: 'Within the last few days fresh difficulties have arisen with reference to Lord Palmerston's conduct of foreign affairs, for he keeps the Queen, his colleagues, his friends, and the party in continual hot water; and on this occasion he seems to have given serious offence to a foreign Power, insomuch that a formal apology is said to be required of him. Yet Lord John has made up his mind to fight through the session in defence of a colleague whose proceedings give him perpetual annoyance.'

Lord Palmerston was succeeded in the Foreign Office by Lord Granville, and no better example of the way in which Palmerston took a reverse can he found than Greville's account of his conduct towards his successor, Earl Granville:

'Yesterday Granville was with Palmerston for three hours. He received him with the greatest cordiality and good-humour. "Ah, how are you, Granville? Well, you have got a very interesting office, but you will find it very laborious; seven or eight hours' work every day will be necessary for the current business, besides the extraordinary and parliamentary, and with less than that you will fall into arrears!" He then entered into a complete history of our diplomacy, gave him every sort of information, and even advice; spoke of the Court without bitterness, and in strong terms of the Queen's "sagacity," ended by desiring Granville would apply to him when he pleased for any information or assistance he could give him. This is very creditable, and, whatever may come after it, very wise, gentlemanlike, becoming, and dignified.'

IX

Drifting into War

L ORD PALMERSTON SOON HAD HIS 'tit-for-tat with John Russell.' In February, 1852, an amendment moved by him to the Militia Bill was carried and Lord John Russell resigned. The Earl of Derby, 'the Rupert of debate,' then formed his first Administration, in which Benjamin Disraeli held office as Chancellor of the Exchequer. A dissolution followed, and Lord Palmerston went to Tiverton to be elected. He was unopposed, and his return on this occasion was the fifth time he was elected member for Tiverton. In the course of a long speech which he made to the electors on the day of election he said he had been threatened with opposition by a man of independent principles. 'I presume the allusion is to principles wholly independent of common sense, justice, and liberality ... I remember to have heard that the Duchess of Gordon, in the time of Mr Pitt, was told by an elderly statesman in regard to something that he himself had done unwisely, "Really, madam, I feel I am growing an old woman," upon which the Duchess replied, "I am glad to hear that that's all, for I really thought you were growing an old man, and that's a much worse thing." Now I say that those men who tell you that because you have had no invasion since the Norman Conquest, you never will have one, and that you need not guard against it, are old men.'

The general election of the year 1852 did not give Earl Derby a majority, and the production of Mr Disraeli's first budget led to his defeat. As a compromise between Lord John Russell on the one hand and Palmerston on the other, the Earl of Aberdeen was entrusted with the duty of forming a Liberal Government, Palmerston consenting to accept the Home Office and Gladstone the Exchequer, Lord John Russell going to the Foreign Office. Palmerston, in a letter to his brother-in-law, dated December 24, 1852, gives the reasons influencing his action. 'The state of the country in all its interests, foreign and domestic, requires a Government as strong as there are elements for making it; and if my aid is thought by Lansdowne and others likely to be useful, I ought not- to let personal feelings stand in the way.' A later sentence in the same letter puts the matter still more clearly. 'I should, if I had persisted in standing aloof, have been left in a little agreeable political solitude.' Palmerston loved office, and threw himself into his new duties with great spirit and energy.

The following letter to his brother William, written April 3, 1853, enables us to see him hard at work in his new harness:

'Ever since the meeting of Parliament I have been living as people do during a contested election, talked to from morning to night, and with no time to do anything. The mere routine business of the Home Office as far as that consists in daily correspondence is very far lighter than that of the Foreign Office; but during a session of Parliament the whole day of the Secretary of State, up to the time when he must go to the House of Commons, is taken up by deputations of all kinds, and interviews with MP's and militia colonels, &c. But, on the whole, it is a much easier office than the Foreign; and, in truth, I really would not on any consideration undertake again an office so unceasingly laborious every day of the year as that of Foreign Affairs.

'I shall be able to do some good in the Home Office. I am shutting up all the graveyards in London, a measure authorised by an Act of last session, and absolutely required for the preservation of the health of the town. There is a company who are going to make two great tunnels under London, fifty feet below the surface, one north, the other south of the Thames, running nearly alongside the river, beginning some way above the town and ending some way below it. These tunnels are to be the receptacles into which all the sewers of London and the drains are to be discharged, so that nothing is to go into the Thames; and the contents of these tunnels are at the point of termination to be dried and converted into manure, to be sold to agriculturists as home-made guano. I shall try to compel at least the tall chimneys to burn their own smoke, and I should like to put down beer-shops, and to let shopkeepers sell beer like oil, or vinegar, or treacle, to be carried home and drunk with wives and children.

'Our session will be long but not dangerous. We shall have to renew the Income Tax and the East India Charter. There are other matters which will take time; but I do not see that another Government is at present possible. The last Cabinet has been too much discredited to be put back again; and Derby, having failed in his experiment to make a Cabinet out of men who knew nothing of the public business, would scarcely like to make another trial with a new set equally ignorant and incapable. Besides, if we were beat by mere numbers, there would be the resource of a dissolution, to which I conclude we should have recourse rather than at once give up our posts. We may have some difficulty next year about Parliamentary Reform, but enough for the year are the troubles thereof. As yet, nothing can be more harmonious than our Coalition Cabinet. I daresay you may have heard at Naples much about our harbouring conspiring refugees.

'The answer I make to those who complain of those matters here is, that a handful of refugees in London cannot arrange a revolution in a foreign country, and send out the plan to be executed off-hand. They must, in the first place, have associates and instruments many thousands in number in the country to which the plan is to be applied, because a revolution cannot be acted by a handful of people. They must have much local knowledge to make their arrangements, and this knowledge, bearing upon circumstances which vary from day to day, is not possessed by men in London, and can only be furnished by men on the spot. Therefore these London conspiracies can do nothing without the co-operation of a great number of people in the foreign country, with whom they must have long and detailed communication either by letters or by messengers. But what are the Governments of the foreign countries about if they cannot, by their policy and their passport system, find out the proceedings of the large mass of these conspirators who are in their own country, and if they cannot intercept the letters and discover and arrest the messengers? It is plain that the practical and real conspiracy is worked out in the foreign country and not in England; and these foreign Governments try to throw upon us a blame which really belongs to them; and if arms and ammunition are sent or provided it is the foreign Government that ought to be able to find that out ...

'The country generally is highly prosperous, trade flourishing, the revenue good, and the emigration having gone just far enough to raise wages to a proper amount without making labour inconveniently scarce. The Irish emigration will, I hope, go on, and it would be a great good thing if a larger number of the Catholic Celts would go off to America, so that their place might be filled by Protestant Anglo-Saxons. This is the kind of operation that is going on. The priests are, of course, furious. Every emigrant is so much out of their pocket. We have a plan in prospect for a general system of drainage of the whole of the valley of the Test, from Whitchurch to Redbridge. I think it will be carried into execution, and if so it will improve the climate as well as the soil ... We had a tea- party for the children of the Romsey School to celebrate Miss Oliphant's successful exertions as schoolmistress for fifty years.'

The 'difficulty next year about Parliamentary Reform' came earlier, and came closer home than he anticipated; for in December, 1852, Lord Palmerston resigned his office of Home Secretary, but on being told that the Government proposals were not final re-entered the Cabinet after a few days' absence. At the time of this crisis the *Times* said: 'Lord Palmerston has not only proved himself as Home Secretary a most efficient administrator, but he has given in a liberal spirit the benefit of his advice and judgment in the discussion of all the important questions of foreign policy which the last twelve months have brought under the consideration of Ministers.'

In this connection it may be of interest to glance for a moment at the objections felt by Lord Palmerston to the Government scheme of reform. He has put them on record with his accustomed clearness, and they form a good standard by which to measure the distance we have since travelled. To those who have lived through the Reform Acts of 1867 and 1884 he appears to crane at very small fences. His views are set forth at length in a memorandum addressed to Lord John Russell, and in a letter to Lord Landsdowne:

'... In considering the subject there are some reflections which naturally occur: is it necessary to make any changes in our representative system? Does the country demand such changes? and what are the changes which, if there be a demand for any, would meet that demand with the least derangement of the existing balance of the Constitution? As to necessity, the real necessity for some changes arises, not from any general demand for them by the country at large, for everybody agrees that no such demand exists. The necessity arises principally, if not solely, from declarations made by you in the House of Commons in former years, without any previous concert or agreement with the other members of your Government. I say this not as a reproach, but as an historical fact, not without some bearing on the course which we have now to pursue, because in proportion to the nature and greatness of the necessity should be the nature and greatness of the measure to be adopted. Still, there is in public opinion a demand for reform, but the reform which most men call for is not so much a general revision of our representative organisation, as a remedy for those abuses of bribery and corruption which were exposed by the proceedings of Election Committees last session.

'Your plan is as to distribution:

1. Disfranchisement of all places having less than 300 electors.
2. Semi-disfranchisement of all under 500.
3. Transfer of seventy seats thus created: half to counties, half to learned bodies, three or four in number, and to large towns.
4. County franchise to be reduced from £50 and occupation to £20.
5. Borough franchise to be reduced from £10 to (I did not hear what).
6. In places having more than two members each elector to vote for two only.
7. Freemen to be disfranchised.

'Now the objection which strikes me as to the general nature and effect of your plan is that it tends without necessity to produce a great derangement in the existing balance of legislative and political power as possessed by the several classes of the community, and to take away a large portion of such power from the aristocracy, the landowners, and the gentry, and to give it over to the manufacturing, commercial, and working classes. Such a transfer seems to me uncalled for and unwise. The last-mentioned classes are strong enough already in Parliament. They ought to be strong and well represented, but their interests are so often separable from the great interests of the country, that I should be sorry to see them become, through a majority in the House of Commons, paramount masters of the destinies of the country, and the present state of things seems to give them power enough for all purposes of good. These remarks apply to the commercial and manufacturing classes. The working men certainly have not much weight, except indirectly, but some of them are electors, and their interests as a class are efficiently cared for by their employers, and by the representatives of the places and counties where they are found in any considerable numbers. Now what I should say about your plan is as follows:

'I agree to the disfranchisement of boroughs under 300. We stand pledged to this by what passed during the progress of the Reform Act. I dissent from the semi-disfranchisement of places under 500. There was no pledge about that. There is no necessity for it. It rests on no principle. It would be a needless derangement of the existing state of things. I think that the confiscated seats of the disfranchised small boroughs ought to be given entirely to counties, to unsettle as little as possible the present balance of power. The seats already confiscated by disfranchisement for corruption would afford the means of giving representation to the learned bodies, and the confiscated seats of one large town could be justly transferred to another large town. The town population is, I believe, already over-represented as compared with the rural population.

The county franchise might safely be reduced, but £30 would be better than £20. I should be very unwilling, in the present uncertain state of things as to what may in a few years be the relative value of money and commodities, to meddle with the borough franchise. If the vast additions annually making to the quantity of the precious metals should materially diminish their value as compared with other things, a house now rated at £8 may soon be rated at £10, and such a change would of itself cause a considerable extension of the franchise to those who do not now enjoy it. Opinions are divided as to the probable effect of the gold discoveries, but certain it is that almost all prices have risen during the last years in almost every country. Time only will show whether this has been the consequence of permanent or of temporary and accidental causes ...

'The scheme of giving electors only two votes for three members deserves consideration but there can be no necessity for, or advantage in, giving additional members to Manchester and such-like places in order to try the principle. I threw out a suggestion at our last meeting that the constituent body might be increased by letting into it classes of men of education and intelligence, and possessed of property not within the description which is now the qualification for a vote. It might be difficult to invent a method of easily ascertaining whether such persons were, at the time of voting, still possessed of the property or income in right of which they might claim to vote, but perhaps this might be contrived, and such men, who must be numerous, would be far better trustees for the nation than working men, whom the late strikes have shown not to be, in many cases, free agents, or masters of their own conduct, but to be the instruments of leaders, who use the men for purposes not those of the men themselves ...

Lord Palmerston wrote again on the same subject to Lord Lansdowne in December, 1853:

'I have had two conversations with Aberdeen on the subject of Russell's proposed Bill, and I have said that there are three points in it to which I cannot agree. These points are the extent of disfranchisement, the extent of enfranchisement, and the addition of the municipal franchise in boroughs to the £10 householders' franchise. My opinion is that a disfranchisement of twenty seats would be amply sufficient, and that all the members so cut off from boroughs ought to be given to counties, or divisions of counties, while those members who belonged to the two boroughs already disfranchised for bribery might be given to the Inns of Court, Stalybridge, and Burnley. I object to a more extensive disfranchisement, and to that addition of members to the Metropolitan boroughs and great towns which would be the necessary result of such more extensive disfranchisement. If hereafter any borough should be disfranchised for bribery, it might be fair to transfer their members to other large towns not now represented, but I cannot be a party to the extensive transfer of representatives from one class to another which would be the consequence of John Russell's plan. I cannot agree to swamp the £10 householders by adding to them the municipal voters, who would comprise all persons rated even to one pound a year, if they could find, as they probably would, some person willing to help them to pay their rates for three years. We should have such an arrangement increase the number of bribable electors, and overpower intelligence and property by ignorance and poverty.

'I have told Aberdeen that I am persuaded that the measure as proposed by John Russell and Graham will not pass through the two Houses of Parliament without material modification, and that I do not choose to be a party to a contest between the two Houses, or to an appeal to the country for a measure which I decidedly disapprove, and that I cannot enter into a career that would lead me into such a position—that, in short, I do not choose to be dragged through the dirt by John Russell. I reminded Aberdeen that on accepting his offer of office I had expressed apprehension both to him and to you that I might find myself differing from my colleagues on the question of Parliamentary Reform. I have thought a good deal on this matter, and should be very sorry to give up my present office at this moment. I have taken a great interest in it, and I have matters in hand which I should much wish to bring to a conclusion. However, I think that the presence in the Cabinet of a person holding the opinions which I entertain as to the principles on which our foreign policy ought to he conducted is useful in modifying the contrary system of policy, which, as I think injuriously to the interest and dignity of the country, there is a disposition in other quarters to pursue, but, notwithstanding all this, I cannot consent to stand forward as one of the authors and supporters of John Russell's sweeping alterations.'

In a letter to Lord Aberdeen (1853) he puts forward the same views:

'There are sometimes occasions in public affairs when the opinions and wishes of the great bulk of the nation are strongly directed to some particular object, and on such occasions it may be wise, and even necessary, for men in public life to surrender their own opinion if contrary to the public wish, and to yield in some degree at least to a current which they are unable to stem. But the present occasion is not one of that kind. The great mass of the intelligent portion of the nation deprecate any material change in the organic arrangements of the House of Commons, though their wishes are strongly set upon some measures which shall prevent the bribery and corruption which have of late so flagrantly prevailed at elections. Therefore, in regard to the organic changes which we may propose, we shall justly be considered not as yielding up our own opinions to a pressure from without, but as proposing to Parliament changes of organisation which on calm consideration we think would he absolutely improvements upon the present state of things.'

In February of the following year he again laid his views before Lord Aberdeen:

'I much wished yesterday to have taken the opinions of the Cabinet on the two points of the proposed Reform Bill in regard to which I circulated a memorandum some time ago. I mean the proposed change in the borough franchise, and the right of voting proposed to be given to anybody who pays £40 a year. That sum was, I think, agreed upon without sufficient consideration. But that which I wish principally to record my protest against is the proposed change in the borough franchise. Its proposed extension to householders rated at £6 will admit, in all probability, about a hundred and fifty thousand voters, or about a quarter of the existing number. These people will be inferior to the £10 in intelligence and independence. They will be comparatively poor, ignorant, and dependent. Their ignorance will prevent them from exercising a sound judgment—their poverty will make them accessible to bribes—their dependence will make them victims of intimidation; and thus while with one hand you are disfranchising freemen because they are venal, and while you are bringing in laws to check bribery and corruption, you are with the other hand laying the foundation for a continuance of those very abuses which you profess to correct. Everybody who knows anything about the working classes will tell you that they are not free agents. The system of organisation which universally prevails among them by means of the Trades Unions gives to their agitating leaders an absolute despotism over the masses. This has been abundantly proved by strikes. The strikers are compelled to refuse to work at a certain rate of wages, on the pretence that those wages are not enough to support them with the present prices of things; and yet other men at work at those very rates are compelled to contribute a portion of those wages towards the support of those who are idle and earning nothing. These £6 voters will, on the one hand, be coerced by their leaders to vote for Chartists and ultra-Radical candidates; and, on the other, will be urged by their employers to vote for some other person. They will be taken between the hammer and the anvil like the Irish peasant, and will cry loudly for ballot as their only protection—or, where the struggle may not arise, they will sell themselves to the highest bidder. Can it be expected that men who murder their children to get £9 to be spent in drink will not sell their vote for whatever they can get for it?

'You may depend upon it that this lowering of the borough franchise is particularly distasteful to the great body of our friends and supporters, and is looked upon with great and general disapprobation. I must be allowed to say that the course which the Government is pursuing in these matters is an error in statesmanship and is at variance with the plainest principles of parliamentary tactics. Wise statesmen do not make great and sweeping changes in the constitutional organisation of their country without some adequate necessity. That necessity may be created by the existence of practical evils which urgently require correction, or by the strong and general desire of the nation for some particular alteration. Neither of these causes of necessity exists in the present case. It will, indeed, be an interposition of that Turkish providence which takes care of men because they cannot take care of themselves if the Government does not sustain some considerable defeat in the progress of these measures through the two Houses of Parliament.'

But while these deliberations were taking place incidents had occurred which led to all thoughts of Reform being postponed for the time. Throughout the year 1853 the policy of the British Cabinet was slowly but surely tending in the direction of war, either because the Prime Minister could not or would not make up his mind as to the policy to be followed. Meanwhile events moved rapidly, and on November 30 the Russian fleet annihilated the Turkish fleet at Sinope. On December so Lord Palmerston addressed the following memorandum to Lord Aberdeen:

'... Will you allow me to repeat in writing what I have more than once said verbally on the state of things between Russia and Turkey? It appears to me that we have two objects in view—the one, to put an end to the present war between those two Powers; the other, to prevent as far as diplomatic arrangements can do so a recurrence of similar differences, and through such differences renewed danger to the peace of Europe. Now it seems plain that, unless Turkey shall be laid prostrate at the feet of Russia by disasters in war, an event which England and France could not without dishonour permit, no peace can be concluded between the contending parties unless the Emperor consents to abandon his demands, to evacuate the Principalities, and to renounce some of the embarrassing stipulations of former treaties, upon which he has founded the pretensions which have been the cause of existing difficulties. To bring the Emperor to agree to this, it is necessary to bring to bear a considerable pressure upon him, and the quarter in which that pressure can at the present be most easily brought to bear is the Black Sea and the countries which border it. In the Black Sea, the combined English, French, and Turkish Squadrons were indisputably superior to the Russian fleet, and are able to give the law to that fleet. What I would strongly recommend, therefore, is that which I proposed some months ago to the Cabinet, namely, that the Russian Government and the Russian admiral at Sebastopol should be informed that, so long as Russian troops occupy the Principalities or hold a position in any other part of the Turkish territory, no Russian ship of war can be allowed to show itself out of port in the Black Sea. You will say that this would be an act of hostility towards Russia, but so is the declaration already made that no Russian ships of war shall be allowed to make any landing or attack on any part of the Turkish territory. The only difference between the two declarations is, that the one already made is incomplete and insufficient for its purpose, and that the other would be sufficient. With regard to the conditions of peace, the only arrangement should be that the treaty to be made between Russia and Turkey should be an ordinary treaty of peace and friendship, and that all stipulations for the Principalities, &c., should be contained in a treaty between the Sultan and the five Powers.'

Then followed his temporary resignation of the Home Office, and the *Morning Post* expresses views which were doubtless very widely held at that time:

'Lord Palmerston throughout has urged a straightforward and honourable policy, and we have every reason to believe that to neglect of his advice the disaster of Sinope is owing.' This event was the first act of the war, begun by the invasion of the harbour of Sinope by the Russian fleet, and the burning of the Turkish war-ships at that port. The *Examiner* also wrote: 'When the public see the backward, lukewarm policy of the Ministry with regard to the Turkish cause, they fancy they perceive the reason why Lord Palmerston conceals the true motive of his resignation, and ascribes it to his objection to the Reform project instead of to his dissatisfaction with the conduct of the Eastern Question.'

The Duke of Argyll has put on record a very lively sketch of both the views and the appearance of his famous colleague at this trying time:

'When the Cabinet of Lord Aberdeen first began to feel that war with Russia was not likely to be averted by negotiations, they began also to consider with care how such a war could be most advantageously conducted. The wildest suggestions and the most passionate incitements abounded in the country. We were urged to rouse the Poles to insurrection, to subsidise the Circassians, and even to attack open and undefended commercial cities. No such schemes could commend themselves to responsible Ministers of any party in the State.

'But from a very early date our attention was fixed on the Crimea, and the great naval station of Sebastopol as the principal point of our attack. The arguments in favour of this course were, indeed, obvious and unanswerable. From Sebastopol came those Russian fleets and expeditions which threatened Constantinople and the Bosphorus. On the other hand, Sebastopol was the most accessible, and the most exposed to our naval power. Nor was it less favourable as the best point of attack for our comparatively limited military forces. If we could secure a safe base for our operations on the coast the utmost might be made of our resources both by sea and land. Further, the defence of Sebastopol would strain to the utmost the resources of Russia, from the vast distances over which her troops must travel. Finally, the main object of the war could be best attained by the destruction of the great naval arsenal which gave Russia the absolute command of the Black Sea.

'Immediately after the final decision had been taken, I was walking one day down to a Cabinet, to be held in Downing Street, from Carlton Terrace. At the foot of the steps from the Duke of York's Column I overtook Lord Palmerston, who at that time lived in Carlton Gardens. Taking his arm and walking with him across the Parade, I began a conversation on the prospects before us, and spoke of the obvious seriousness of the task to which we were committed. To my surprise he not only spoke with unhesitating conviction of the wisdom of the selection made (of which I had no doubt), but with the most absolute confidence of an easy and certain success. I was much struck with his sanguine and optimistic tone. He said there was no reason to doubt the issue—that Sebastopol was so situated that it could be practically invested it was a maxim in military science that places which could be invested must ultimately fall—that it was a mere question of time and of endurance, &c., &c.

'His manner in saying all this was almost "jaunty," the result, it seemed to me,—of natural temperament rather than of more reasoned conviction. I was much struck with it at the time, and often 'looked back to it afterwards in the midst of operations which strained our resources to the very utmost. Confidence in general maxims, such as those cited by Lord Palmerston, is never quite justified, unless all the conditions which make them applicable can with certainty be known. I did not feel that this knowledge was altogether in our possession. In the final result he was right, but only after a triumph over dangers and difficulties which he did not foresee. A sanguine and confident temper was in the nature of the man. He was then sixty-nine years old, and I was only thirty-one, yet I could not help feeling that I was in some ways the elder of the two.'

X

Prime Minister for the First Time

Lord Palmerston had passed his seventieth year when the Premiership came to him for the first time. On the fall of the Coalition Government the Queen sent for Lord Derby, and upon his failure for Lord John Russell. Palmerston was willing at the express request of her Majesty to serve once more under his old chief; but Clarendon and many of the Whigs not unnaturally positively refused to do so. Palmerston finally undertook and successfully achieved the task of forming a Government out of the somewhat heterogeneous elements at his command. Lord Clarendon continued at the Foreign Office, and Gladstone was still Chancellor of the Exchequer. The War Department was reorganised, the office of Secretary *at* War disappearing, and being finally merged in that of Secretary of State for War. Although Palmerston objected to Roebuck's Committee, he was practically compelled to accept it, and this led to the resignation of Gladstone, Graham, and Herbert; their places being taken by Sir G. C. Lewis, Sir Charles Wood, and Lord John Russell.

It looked at first as though Lord Palmerston's optimistic views would be justified by facts. The allied troops of England and France landed in the Crimea, September 14, 1854. A few days afterwards the battle of the Alma was won, and on October the news of the fall of Sebastopol arrived. But very speedily all this was changed. Sebastopol had not fallen, but it rapidly became evident that the most scandalous inefficiency characterised the administration of the War Department. Sickness swept off more than the enemy. Public indignation grew apace. Instantly upon the meeting of Parliament, January 23, 1855, Mr Roebuck gave notice to move for a committee of inquiry upon the condition of the army before Sebastopol, and the conduct of the Government Departments. Lord John Russell, in one of the least creditable acts of his public life, immediately resigned, thus leaving his colleagues in the lurch. Roebuck's motion was carried by 305 to 148, and on February 14, 1855, Lord Aberdeen resigned.

Lord Palmerston wrote to the Emperor of the French, February 1855:

'Appelé par la Reine ma Souveraine au poste que maintenant j'occupe, je m'empresse de satisfaire au besoin que je sens d'exprimer à Votre Majesté la grande satisfaction que j'éprouve à me trouver en rapport plus direct avec le gouvernement de Votre Majesté. L'alliance qui unit si heureusement la France et l'Angleterre, et qui promet des résultats si avantageux pour toute l'Europe, prend son origine dans la loyauté, la franchise, et la sagacité de Votre Majesté; et Votre Majesté pourra toujours compter sur la loyauté et la franchise du Gouvernement Anglais. Et si Votre Majesté avait jamais une communication à nous faire, sur des idées non encore assez mûries pour être le sujet de dépêches officielles, je m'estimerais très heureux en recevant une telle communication de la part de Votre Majesté.

Nous allons mettre un peu d'ordre à notre camp devant Sébastopol, et en cela nous tâcherons d'imiter le bel exemple qui nous est montré par le camp Français. A quelque chose, cependant, malheur est bon; et le mauvais état de l'armée Anglaise à donné aux braves et généreux Français l'occasion de prodiguer à leurs frères d'armes des soins qui ont excité la plus vive reconnaissance tant en Angleterre qu'à Balaclava. J'ai l'honneur d'être, Sire, &c. PALMERSTON.

This letter shows Lord Palmerston's desire that the Government should have informal communications as well as official relations with the French monarch—a principle he always acted on, and one which, as we have already noted, often occasioned anxiety among his friends and colleagues.

His views upon the state of things at the seat of war were very clear: 'With regard to the army abroad, it must be obvious to anyone who has attended to the course of events that a large part of the sufferings and the sickness of the army in the Crimea has arisen from causes which might have been prevented by better arrangements and greater activity and care on the part of the heads of the staff. It has also been determined to establish a certain number of hospital ships, capable of conveying 500 sick in each, and that one of these ships shall every ten days leave Balaclava and Scutari, bringing home its cargo of wounded and sick, and that such ship shall immediately return to Scutari or Balaclava loaded with hospital stores and other things required for the men in the hospitals and the army. It has also been determined that a Commission shall be sent out to inquire into the Commissariat and Harbour arrangements. We have made arrangements for procuring from the small-arm manufacturers of the United States 100,000 Minié rifles.'

Lord Palmerston, in February, 1855, stated that he had 'received an important letter from the Emperor of the French, in which the Emperor announces his intention of going to the Crimea for the purpose of driving back the Russians from Simpheropol, and then falling back to take Sebastopol. He proposes to accomplish the first operation with an army of 77,000 men—French and Sardinians—leaving 66,000 English and French and Turks to maintain the siege. The condition is that we should find the means of transporting to the Crimea 10,000 French, 15,000 Sardinians, and 3,000 horses; but, whether the military operation he deemed practicable or expedient or not, the Emperor's personal visit to the Crimea seems wholly unnecessary for its accomplishment, and might be attended with most lamentable consequences.'

The Emperor was subsequently dissuaded with difficulty from paying this visit to the seat of war.

On the death of the Emperor Nicholas Lord Palmerston wrote: 'This may or may not produce important changes in the state of affairs. It is probable that the Grand Duke Hereditary will succeed quietly, notwithstanding the notion that a doubt would be started whether he, as son of the Grand Duke Nicholas, would not be superseded by his younger brother, born son of the Czar. It is possible that the new Emperor may revert to that peaceful policy which he was understood to advocate in the beginning of these transactions; but he may feel bound to follow out the policy of his father, and may be impelled by the headstrong ambition of his brother Constantine. At all events, this change at St Petersburg should not for the present slacken the proceedings and arrangements of the Allies.

Negotiations for peace had already been commenced, but meanwhile the war was prosecuted with new vigour. In March, 1855, the Prime Minister thus sketches his policy in the Baltic:

'It seems to be impossible to do more in the Baltic than blockade the Russian ports and fleet, for which purpose the twenty sail of the line and the five which the Emperor will add to them appear to be sufficient, but not more than sufficient, seeing that the Russians have twenty-seven sail of the line in the Baltic, and that accidents might happen in crossing to disable for a time some ships of the allied fleets. The Russian fleet is all concentrated at Cronstadt. There would consequently be no use in attacking Revel or Sveaborg, which are both strongly fortified. A successful attack would only knock down some stone walls, which, as the places could not be occupied or kept, would soon be rebuilt, and the attacking squadron would necessarily sustain much damage. An unsuccessful attack would of course be a disaster. Further, neither we nor the French could well spare or transport to the Baltic troops enough to accomplish any important operation. It seems, therefore, to be good policy that England and France should direct all their efforts to the Crimea, where the real battle is to be fought, and that, till success is obtained there, it would be unwise to weaken the exertions in that quarter by attempting anything else important elsewhere. This reasoning, of course, does not exclude operations in the Sea of Azoff or along the coast of Circassia, if favourable opportunity present itself.

A month later he criticises the Emperor Napoleon's plan of campaign:

'It seems to me that we should say to Lord Raglan that he should enter into cordial concert and dispassionate consultation with Canrobert on the subject of this plan, and that our wish is that whatever may seem on full consideration to be best should be undertaken; that we are of opinion with the Emperor that Sebastopol cannot be taken until it is fully invested; and that it cannot be fully invested unless the Russian covering army is driven away from its present position, from which it communicates with the town. That for this purpose it seems advisable to divide the aggregate force into three armies, as proposed by the Emperor, of which one should maintain the siege, while another moves forward to complete the investment; the third making a diversion, which would be a feint, to draw off the Russians from their position near the town, or a real attack on their rear, according to circumstances, and especially according to the relative force of the army making the diversion and the Russian force by which it might be opposed.

'The main question on which the generals would have to deliberate would be the direction in which, and the point from which, this diversion should be made. The Emperor strongly recommends the Alashta as the starting point, and Simpheropol or Batchisarai as the object. Another opinion is that Eupatoria would be the best basis of operations for the army of diversion, and that from thence it should march on Simpheropol, or take in the rear the Russian force to the north of Sebastopol; and that, advancing along the line of coast, it should keep up its communications with a squadron of the Allies which should accompany its march. To this plan the Emperor states objections. These objections will of course be well weighed by the generals. A third plan is that the third army of operation should not be embarked and transported anywhere by sea, but should march away from the general centres of operations at Kamiesch and Balaclava, and get to Batchisarai by a road leading to the eastward of McKenzie's Farm. We must leave it to the generals on the spot to determine which of these three plans affords the best prospect of success, and is the most easily executed. Whichever plan, however, is adopted, it ought to be put into execution as soon as the whole of the reinforcements arrive, and the troops intended for the two armies of operation are ready to take the field.'

There was much discussion on these proposals, and Lord Palmerston canvassed them in other letters in full, insisting on as much concentration as possible, and arguing in general in favour of only taking up a strong position to the rear of the town, and maintaining the siege along the southern lines we had occupied with our allies.

Lord Palmerston, meanwhile, watched with a steady gaze the negotiations then going forward at Vienna for peace with Russia, and French co-operation in this respect, and consequent difficulties:

'I do not see that Lord John, the English plenipotentiary at the Conference, is in any degree bound to follow the example of M. Drouyn de l'Huys. Drouyn with his own hand wrote down, after full deliberation with us, the conditions which the two Governments were to make their ultimatum, and the rejection of which by Russia was to be followed by a formal breaking off of the Conference negotiations. But no sooner were those conditions rejected by Russia that he hastily catches up a totally different plan proposed by Austria, and pins his own Government and our plenipotentiary to that different plan; and now, because it is rejected by his own Government, he breaks off his official relations with that Government and drags our plenipotentiary after him. As to Lord John's intention, all that one can say is that I should think it was the first instance in which a plenipotentiary, having undertaken a negotiation on instructions founded on principles of which he approved, turned round upon his Government, and after the plan which he had been instructed to press had failed, should turn round upon his employers and endeavour to force upon them a plan totally different from that which he had undertaken to propose. Any objection Lord John urges applies with tenfold force to his intention to resign (like M. Drouyn de l'Huys), because his resignation must necessarily be followed by a full parliamentary discussion of the details and merits and demerits of the plan upon the rejection of which he means to found his resignation. This will drive us to argue against his plan, and will compel us to commit ourselves on many points which it would be better to let stand open.'

In April Lord Palmerston had already spoken of the Austrian proposal adopted by M. Drouyn de l'Huys, even with his pretended modification, as 'only to be described in the concise terms by which it was said that, instead of making to cease the preponderance of Russia in the Black Sea, it would perpetuate and legalise that preponderance, and, instead of establishing a secure and permanent peace, it would only establish a prospective case for war. M. Drouyn would sanction a Russian fleet in the Black Sea to any amount short by one ship of the number existing in 1853. Such an arrangement would, in my opinion, be alike dangerous and dishonourable, and as to the accompanying alliance with Austria for the future defence of Turkey, and for making war with Russia if she were to raise her Black Sea fleet up to the amount of 1853, what reason is there to believe that Austria, who shrinks from war with Russia now that the army of Russia has been much reduced by losses, now that her forces are divided and occupied elsewhere than on the Austrian frontier, and now that England and France are actually in the field with large armies supported by great fleets—what reason is there to believe that this same Austria would be more ready to make war four or five years hence, when the army of Russia shall have repaired its losses, and shall be more concentrated to attack Austria, when the Austrian army shall have been reduced to its peace establishment, and when the peace establishments of England and France, withdrawn within their home stations, shall be less ready to co-operate with Austria in war?'

Lord Palmerston, no less than later Prime Ministers, found the *Times* a source of trouble, and he did not hesitate to express his views upon the conduct of that paper in very plain terms:

'Though the *Times* does and intends to do much mischief, yet that mischief is often very temporary and much limited. That paper often takes a line in hopes of being followed by public opinion, but when it finds that public opinion goes another way, it changes its course and follows public opinion. What the managers aim at, above all, is to get a great circulation for their paper, and that is not to be obtained by running long against the feelings and opinions of the mass of the nation. Thus it was that the *Times,* having begun by taking the part of Russia, has now become one of the most insolent antagonists of Russia; and there have been many other instances of similar changes of language as to men and things. I have had as much reason as most people to complain of the *Times*, for from the time when I first went to the Foreign Office, for some reason or other which I never could discover, the *Times* has been animated by undeviating hostility, personal and political, towards me, and I have never known from whom or from whence that hostility proceeded. Within the last fortnight the *Times* has in some degree changed its tone, with apologies for doing so, merely because the capture of Sebastopol has turned public opinion strongly in favour of the existing Government. But before long the paper will probably revert more or less to its former course.'

Lord Palmerston was, of course, most intimately acquainted with the policies of the various Courts with regard to the peace negotiations, and also with the diplomatists entrusted with their execution. This renders his letters at this time most valuable as a means of understanding the tricky and intricate manoeuvres which he ultimately foiled. On October 9, 1855, he wrote to Lord Clarendon:

'It is of course to be foreseen that between this time and the spring the Russian Government will make as vigorous efforts to escape the further pressure and defeats which another campaign is sure to bring on as they have made to maintain themselves in Sebastopol, and it must be our business to baffle them. With Nesselrode's two daughters, one at Paris, the other at Brussels; with Morny and all the other Russian agents acting on the French Government; and with Vienna and Berlin co-operating—we shall find all our steadiness and skill required to avoid being drawn into a peace which would disappoint the just expectations of the country, and leave unaccomplished the real objects of the war.

'I don't see any good that could result from our proceeding now to discuss with the French Government the terms of peace; if we want to discuss anything, let it rather be the best way of carrying on the war. Whatever terms of peace we might agree with the French Government to demand, those terms would in a week be made known to the Russian Government, and would be represented as overtures coming from us. If indeed, those terms were sufficiently satisfactory to us, and if they were in consequence rejected by Russia, no great harm would be done, except that we should be attacked for insincerity in pretending to want peace while asking terms which, it would be said, we knew Russia would not accept. The fact is, as you said the other day, Russia has not yet been beat enough to make peace possible at the present moment.

'With regard to the conditions sketched out by Walewski, I should say that the first point requires more than mere changes of detail. The guarantee of the five Powers was a vicious principle, because whatever powers of interference that guarantee could confer on the five would be practically exercised by Russia and Austria, and matters would be worse instead of better. The only way of cutting off the Austrian and Russian interference in the internal affairs of the Principalities would be that which we have pressed on the Porte—*viz.* that the Sultan should give the Principalities a good constitution, to be previously agreed to by England and France. Walewski's plan of requiring Russia to give up the Delta of the Danube, and to restore it to Turkey, would be the most effectual; but we must have brought some heavy pressure to hear upon Russia to make her consent to this course. As to the third point, the idea of proposing to Russia now that she should have in the Black Sea four liners and four frigates, besides other smaller vessels, is childish. We ought to insist on the neutralisation plan, and if we get hold of the Crimea we ought well to reflect before we give it back at all to Russia. The Turks would be quite able to keep it, at all events till succour should arrive, especially if Russia had no war-fleet on the Black Sea. The way in which Walewski proposes to settle the fourth point is certainly the best, and if the non-Mussulman population were put upon a footing of perfect equality with the Mussulmans, foreign Powers might, all of them, give up their respective rights, real or claimed, of protective interference, retaining of course that which they could not be deprived of, the right of diplomatic representation on important matters in which their co-religionists were concerned, such representation being no longer founded upon any right of interference.

'As to money payments to be exacted from Russia, I doubt the advisability of making such a demand. The Russian Government would probably resist it, just as much as it would the cession of any part of Russian territory, which might have been wrested from Russia during war; and such a payment, while the burthen of it would fall on the luckless nation and not on the offending government, would have only a temporary effect in restraining Russia, whereas the wresting from her permanently particular portions of territory which are in her hands, sallying points for attacks upon her neighbours, would lastingly diminish her means and power of aggression. Such would be the effect of taking the Crimea away from Russia while the neutrality plan was established for the Black Sea. Georgia and Circassia taken from Russia would be a better security than a large money payment. If you leave in the hands of Russia the advanced posts from whence she can make invasions and attacks, even although you take money from her, she will be sure, when she wants to do so, to find money enough to make those posts available for her purposes. If you take away from her those advanced posts, no money can enable her to regain them except by war, which the loss of them disables her from waging with the same advantage.

'Walewski's notions about Poland deserve to be borne in mind, and it would be desirable to act upon them if a fitting state of things should enable us to do so, but at present we are not in a condition to make the demand; and he might be told that if he wishes to re-establish any former condition of things in any part of Poland, he must pave the way by a vigorous pressure upon Russia, and by turning a deaf ear to the Russian agents and partisans by whom he is and will continue to be surrounded and beset. We know what are the terms of peace which would accomplish the real objects of the war, but we have not yet placed ourselves by successes in war in a condition to entitle us to demand those conditions as the price of peace.'

To Count Persigny, the French Ambassador in London, he wrote in November, 1855:

'Mon cher Comte,—Je vous ai écrit bien fort de la hâte, et je pars àt l'instant pour Windsor, mais je désire ajouter deux mots mon billet d'hier soir. D'après notre Constitution et notre régime parlementaire le pouvoir exécutif ne doit jamais faire une démarche aussi importante que celle dont il s'agit sans avoir des pièces officielles à produire au Parlement, afin d'être à même d'expliquer clairement ce qui a été proposé à l'Angleterre, par quels motifs la proposition a été appuyée, et queues ont été les raisons qui ont conseillé son adoption. Mais jusqu'à present nous n'avons rien de tout cela. Il y a eu à Vienne une negotiation à laquelle nous n'avons pas pris part; on a signé—du moins paragraphé—un protocole pour nous, mais sans nous. On nous communique confidentiellement ce protocole paragraphé, à prendre ou à laisser, en nous disant qu'il faut ou le registrer ou l'accepter immédiatement, bon ou mauvais, sans en discuter la rédaction et les détails. Cette manière d'agir dans une affaire tellement grave ne nous convient pas. Nous souhaitons nous conformer aux désirs de l'Empereur, mais il faut que nous soyons en règle vis-à-vis de notre Parlement, et nous ne pouvons pas souscrire à une Proposition de Paix à être faite en notre nom à la Russie sans que nous soyons entièrement d'accord et sur la forme et sur la substance d'une telle proposition. Il est donc indispensable que nous ayons une proposition par écrit, dont nous puissions bien examiner la rédaction, avant de pouvoir donner à l'Autriche l'autonisation qu'elle nous demande de parler à la Russie en notre nom. Je dis parler en notre nom, parce que, malgré que l'Autriche doit s'approprier la démande qu'elle voudrait faire à Pétersbourg, elle se propose de dire qu'elle sait d'avance que sa proposition serait adoptée par l France et l'Angleterre si elle venait d'être acceptée par la Russie. La nation anglaise serait enchantée d'une bonne paix qui assurait les objets de la guerre, mais plutôt que d'être entrainee à signer une paix à des conditions insuffisantes elle préférerait continuer la guerre sans d'autres allies que la Turquie, et elle se sent tout à fait en état de soutenir le fardeau et de se tirer ainsi d'affaire. Soumettez, je vous prie, ces observations à Walewski.

In February, 1856, he wrote the following vigorous description of the state of Russia:

'If it should turn out that the British Plenipotentiaries should be left alone in the Conference, all the others siding with Russia, that would be a very awkward state of things, and would require serious consideration, But that does not at present appear to be likely, and it is much more probable that the Russians will give way. They will not, perhaps, do so at once, but will suspend the conferences, and say they must refer to St Petersburg, and in the meantime will try the effect of intrigue, cajolery, and menace; but if the Allies are firm, being, as they are, clearly and indisputably in the right, the opinion we have heard from Russia will most probably be verified, and Russia will and must give way. What they say varies according to times, places, and persons. Russia is in great exhaustion. She has not more than 400,000 men for her whole line from Finland to Georgia fit to go into action, and her supplies of all kinds are deficient. The limit placed on the armistice is a screw put upon her, and if she does not yield before the end of March, that epoch will most likely bring her to terms. If not, the contemplated operations in the Crimea cannot fail to be successful. I saw yesterday an intelligent person just returned from Paris. He says that the Emperor is known to be firm in alliance with us—that the Ministers are Stock Exchange gamblers the Orleanists and Legitimists the open partisans of Russia—that in society in Paris the Russians are made much of, and the Austrians neglected that the *bourgeoisie* do not share the peace-at-all-price feeling of the *salons* they speak openly of the corruption of those in power, and, though glad to have peace, would not buy it by a sacrifice of national honour—that the army would prefer a continuance of the war—that men for the army are abundant, and large numbers of soldiers whose term of service has expired have enlisted again for a second period. His conclusion is that the Emperor would find no difficulty anywhere but among some of his own Ministers in going on with the war if peace cannot be had on acceptable conditions.'

The month of March was occupied with negotiations for the settlement of peace, Lord Clarendon being the British representative at the Conference held in Paris. The Emperor of the French being very anxious to conclude peace, 'it was determined,' as Lord Palmerston said, 'to inform Lord Clarendon by telegraph that his arrangements were approved of, and that he might yield to the impatience of the Emperor and the members of the Congress and sign the treaty. It is proposed that the Tower and the Park guns shall not be fired until Monday morning. Lord Clarendon has also been told that the peace being made to begin from the exchange of ratifications, which is the simplest plan, the armistice should be formally prolonged to a time sufficiently distant to cover the exchange of ratifications, which may be expected to take place in about three weeks ... We must congratulate ourselves upon an arrangement which effects a settlement that is satisfactory for the present, and which will probably last for many years to come, of questions full of danger to the best interests of Europe. Greater and more brilliant successes by land and sea might probably have been accomplished by the Allies if the war had continued, but any great and important additional security against future aggression by Russia could only have been obtained by severing from Russia large portions of her frontier territory, such as Finland, Poland, and Georgia; and although by great military and financial efforts and sacrifices those territories might for a time have been occupied, Russia must 'have been reduced' to the lowest state of internal distress before her Emperor would have been brought to put his name to a treaty of peace finally surrendering his sovereignty over those extensive countries ; and to have continued the war long enough for those purposes would have required greater endurance than was possessed by our Allies, and might possibly have exhausted the goodwill of our own people.'

The Treaty of Paris was signed on March 30, 1856, and thus came to an end a war which cost England 25,000 lives and which added £50,000,000 to the National Debt. How little it accomplished in the way of putting any permanent check upon Russian aggression the events of the last fifteen years very clearly show.

In the usual shower of rewards and decorations that follow a war, Lord Palmerston's share was the Garter. Upon its receipt in April, 1856, he wrote the following letter to the Queen:

'Viscount Palmerston is unable to express in words the gratification and thankfulness which he feels upon the receipt of your Majesty's most gracious and unexpected communication. The utmost of his ambition has been, so to perform the duties of the high position in which your Majesty has been pleased to place him, as to prove himself not unworthy of the confidence with which your Majesty has honoured him; and the knowledge that your Majesty has found no reason to be dissatisfied with your choice and that his endeavours properly to discharge his duties to your Majesty and the country have met with your Majesty's approval, would of itself be an ample reward for any labour or anxiety with which the performance of those duties may have been attended; and therefore the gracious communication which he has this morning received from your Majesty will be preserved by him as in his eyes still more valuable even than the high honour which it announces your Majesty's intention to confer on him. That high and distinguished honour Viscount Palmerston will receive with the greatest pride, as a public mark of your Majesty's gracious approbation, and he begs to be allowed to say that the task which he and his colleagues have had to perform has been rendered comparatively easy by the enlightened views which your Majesty has taken of all the great affairs in which your Majesty's empire has been engaged, and by the firm and steady support which in all these important transactions your Majesty's servants have received from the Crown.'

Early in 1857, in consequence of the high-handed policy pursued by Lord Palmerston towards China in what was known as 'the affair of the lorcha "Arrow,"' Cobden moved what was practically a vote of censure. This was carried by a majority of sixteen votes. Palmerston at once dissolved Parliament, and in the ensuing General Election scored a great triumph. John Bright, Milner Gibson, and Cobden all lost their seats.

'The results of the General Election,' Palmerston wrote in April, 1857, 'have in the aggregate been most satisfactory. Many objectionable members of the last House of Commons have been thrown out, and though a few men who have been now elected would have been better away, yet on the whole the composition of the new members is good, and there are in the present House of Commons mere gentlemen and more men of character than has usually been the case.'

In June, 1857, the news of the Indian Mutiny reached England. Sir Colin Campbell instantly started to take chief command, and strong bodies of troops were hurried to that distant part of the world. Into the details of that famous story we have no space to enter. We can but give two or three characteristic extracts from the Prime Minister's correspondence.

On a proposal to enlist foreign troops for India, Lord Palmerston wrote: 'I am strongly of opinion that we ought to win this innings against the Sepoys off our own bat. We all know how much the reputation and standing of Austria suffered by the necessity in which she found herself of asking or of receiving assistance from Russia to put down her revolted subjects in Hungary; and a Power which cannot maintain order within its own territories by its own means, may regain its territories by foreign aid, but inevitably sinks in public estimation. As regards the struggle in which we are now engaged in India, my view is not gloomy. I feel perfectly confident that we shall by our own means re-establish our authority in India, and there cannot surely be a doubt that we shall stand far higher as a nation by doing so than if we were to have recourse to the help of foreigners to bring us through. I send you a note showing that, whilst people said we should get too or at most 200 recruits a week in August, we have in that month raised 2,500 recruits, and I doubt not that in this and in the other months from this time to June and July next our success will be much greater. No doubt we shall lose many men by climate and disease, but not so many as some people expect. We are not going to enter into a great campaign against a regular army in the field; our troops will have to hunt down and exterminate bands of mutineers without magazines, resources, commanders, head-quarters, or any of those foundations on which armies are built, and our Government in India will be able to supply them with means and assistance of all kinds to render movement as little fatiguing as possible, and climate as little injurious as may be. The cool season is coming on, and the chief operations will be in the northern part of India, where the climate is more favourable than in the south to European constitutions.'

This was a cheery note sounded in a dark time of depression!

Again, a little later: 'Delhi cannot be taken till reinforcements shall have reached the army before that place; and General Havelock with an inadequate force, having to choose between relieving Agra or Lucknow, or punishing Nana Sahib, must have left two of those objects unaccomplished. But when Delhi shall have been taken the character of the operations will change, for the mutineers, without a base of operations, and without stores and money, will be unable to continue a contest in the field, and those who may shut themselves up in fortified places will only render their capture and punishment the more certain. Scattered bands pf marauders may prowl about the country, but they must live by plunder, and the people whom they rob will take part against them. Our chief difficulty will be to get from place to place in pursuit of these bands, and to catch them and bring them to justice.'

The following letter shows that the sanguine spirit of Lord Palmerston stood high as ever:

'I am sorry to have received an account of the extension of the mutiny among the native troops in India. But I have no fear of its results. The bulk of the European force is stationed on the north-west frontier, and is therefore within comparatively easy reach of Delhi, and about five or six thousand European troops will have returned to Bombay from Persia. It does, however, seem to be advisable to send off at once the force, amounting to nearly 8,000 men, now under orders for embarkation for India, and when the despatches arrive, about the middle of next week, it will be seen whether any further reinforcements will be required. The extent of the mutiny seems to indicate some deeper cause than that which was ascribed to the first insubordination. The cause may be, as some allege, the apprehension of the Hindoo priests that their religion is in danger by the progress of civilisation in India, or it may be some hostile foreign agency.'

The direct result of the Indian Mutiny was the reorganization of the whole system of government in that part of the world. It was evident to all that the days of 'John Company' were numbered; it was not quite so clear what form of control could best take its place. Lord Palmerston, in October, 1857, placed upon record his idea of the best form the Imperial Government of India may take:

'It is my strong personal opinion that the present double government of India ought not to continue, and it is my belief that the nation at large is prepared for a change. We should introduce a measure for the abolition of the Board of Control, the Court of Directors, and the Court of Proprietors, and appoint a Secretary of State for India, to be assisted by one or two under-secretaries, who should be capable of sitting in either House of Parliament, and should be political officers changing with the Government, and they should be assisted by a Council of non-political men, possibly four in number, who should not sit in Parliament, and should not change with changes of Government, but should be in the position of the Permanent Under Secretaries of the four Secretaries of State, with the condition that no one should be appointed who has not served in India in a civil or military capacity. There will, of course, be much opposition on the part of all persons connected with the India Company, and the Opposition in Parliament might take up their cause, and the matter therefore, will require to be well weighed.'

A Bill embodying this policy was brought before the House of Commons in February, 1858; it was carried by the unexpectedly large majority of one hundred and forty-five.

Lord Palmerston at this juncture seemed to stand in a sure place. He was at the head of a Government supported by a large majority, and he was himself at the very height of his personal popularity; and yet in a few days he was suddenly hurled from power.

On January 14, 1858, an attempt was made to assassinate Napoleon III by a gang of desperadoes, headed by Orsini, whose head-quarters had previously been in London. Not without some reason it was felt in France that such men ought not to be able to find shelter in this country, and the French Minister was ordered to make representations to that effect. Lord Palmerston, always anxious to cultivate the good feeling of the French nation, desired to pass a measure which should give to the British Government the power to banish from England any foreigner conspiring in Britain against the life of a foreign sovereign, designing thereby to meet the wishes of the Emperor of the French, who had been deeply moved by the attempts on his life made by Orsini and others. An unfortunate outburst of vituperation against England in the French press, and the repetition of such language by officers of the French army who were received by the Emperor when they waited on him as a deputation, aroused very angry English feeling. Lord Palmerston had already introduced the Bill he desired to pass, and it had been read the first time by a majority of two hundred.

But the foolish action of the French papers changed entirely the current of popular opinion. Lord Derby saw his advantage. An amendment to the second reading, which was practically a vote of censure, was carried against Lord Palmerston, and to his own surprise no less than to that of the country, he was obliged to resign. Lord Derby succeeded to Palmerston's vacant office, and after a quiet summer the ex-Premier visited Napoleon at Compiègne, and enjoyed the stag-hunting and the other sports at that charming country place, and said of his hosts: 'They were all very civil and courteous, and one evening, while a dance was going on, the Emperor walked up and down with me in a neighbouring room, and told me of his ideas in reference to an improvement he wished to carry out in the French franchise. He desired that, instead of universal suffrage, the right of voting should only be permitted to married men. Men who are not married, he said, do not have the same sentiments in regard to their country as do those who are married, and they have a greater stake in the welfare of their country. Moreover, such a limitation of voting power to married men would exclude the soldiers and also the priests, and those classes ought to be excluded. I answered that I thought that property of some kind ought to be the real basis for the suffrage, and while many bachelors would always be possessed of property, married men might have no property.'

Lord Derby's second Ministry was wrecked upon the fatal rock of Reform early in 1859, and at once appealed to the country. At Tiverton, Lord Palmerston was again returned without opposition. As no specimen of his hustings manner has been given in these pages, a little of the oft-repeated 'chaff' that was exchanged between him and a Radical butcher of that place may be quoted. Rowcliffe, for this was the man's name, was always present at the open-air speaking at Tiverton to give Lord Palmerston a 'bit of his mind,' but the old Minister always got the best of the encounter. Rowcliffe this time declared Lord Palmerston was a downright Tory, and the best representative the Tories could possibly have. He hoped his lordship would answer his questions in an honest manner. Lord Palmerston said 'he was delighted to find that his old friend, however far advanced in years, retained that youthful vigour which he possessed when first he knew him, and with his vigour he had retained also his prejudices and opinions. (Laughter and a cry of "No chaff") His friend asked for a straightforward answer, and he would give him one. He totally disagreed with him in almost all his opinions. (Laughter.) He thought the day would never come when he and Mr Rowcliffe would agree in political faith. (Much laughter.) His friend asked him what he thought on many points. In the first place he would say he was opposed to the ballot. He was against manhood suffrage. (Rowcliffe: "How far will you go with the suffrage?") He would give a straightforward answer to that. He would not tell him. (Laughter.) He held it was his duty after the confidence they had reposed in him to act according to his judgment in any measure relating to Reform. (Cheers.) He hoped that the political difference between his friend and himself would not alter their private friendship. (Much laughter.) He was sorry to disagree with his friend, but no man could agree with everybody. The man who did agree with everybody was not worth having anybody to agree with him. (Cheers and laughter.)'

XI

Prime Minister a Second Time

T HE ELECTION OF 1859 FAILED to give the Conservatives a majority,
and soon after the opening of the session they were defeated upon
a vote of want of confidence moved by Lord Hartington. Earl Granville
was commissioned by the Queen to form a Ministry, because her Majesty
felt that 'to make so marked a distinction as is implied in the choice of
one or other as Prime Minister of two statesmen so full of years and honour as Lord Palmerston and Lord John Russell would be a very invidious
and unwelcome task.' Each of these veterans was willing to serve under
the other, but neither would follow the lead of a third. And so Granville
failed, and to Palmerston was entrusted the task. He succeeded in forming what was considered the strongest Ministry of modern times, so far as
the individual ability of its members was concerned. Russell went to the
Foreign Office and Gladstone to the Exchequer. Thus, at the age of sev-
enty-five, Lord Palmerston once again assumed the burden of government
and the leadership of the House of Commons.

During these political changes at home, the memorable battles of
Magenta and Solferino had been fought in Northern Italy, and early in
July France concluded a provisional treaty with Austria. These events had
an all-powerful influence upon Italian politics, and were matters at this
time of daily concern to Lord Palmerston. As heretofore, we give his views
in his own words.

In June, 1859, Lord Palmerston wrote:

'The future condition of political existence to be enjoyed by the
Lombards and Venetians, and by the Italians generally, ought to be

determined by the natives themselves. In what manner the national will should in each case be ascertained will be a matter for future consideration. The fancied interests of other States out of and beyond the Italian Peninsula ought not to control the Italian will. But what are the interests of England in this matter, and how ought our wishes and moral influence to be directed? It is surely for the interests of England that there should be created in Northern Italy a State as independent as possible of foreign dictation, and as likely as possible to consult its own interests, which would lie in commerce and peace. But the weaker a State is, the more dependent it is on its neighbours; the stronger it is, the more able it is to have a policy of its own. It seems, then, to be for our interest that there should be in Northern Italy a State as considerable, and therefore as strong, as circumstances will permit; and such a State must be built upon the present kingdom of Sardinia.

'I can see no danger to English interests in the annexation of Venice to such a State ; on the contrary, a State possessing Genoa and Venice would of necessity make commerce its vital principle, and having two seaports, both of which might, in case of war with England, be blockaded by British squadrons, such a State would have a double inducement against a rupture with England. How far south the new Sardinian territory should go must depend upon events, but I think it is probable that Parma and Modena at all events would be included, and possibly Tuscany. I have doubts as to the opinion expressed that no English Minister ought to sign a treaty of peace that does not provide efficient reforms for the States of the Church. It is most desirable that such reforms should be made, but the making of them might probably be left to the Italians themselves, if all foreign interference were withdrawn.'

France, apparently without any real desire for it, proposed British mediation between France and Austria in July 1859, and upon this proposal Lord Palmerston expressed himself as under:

'Neutrality between belligerents means, in its proper sense, abstinence from giving to either party assistance in carrying on the war, but it does not preclude good offices or mediation with a view to the restoration of peace, and, in fact, it is only a neutral Power that can advantageously perform those functions. But a mediator, to be useful, must not merely be content with transmitting from one party to the other propositions and answers, but should accompany those communications with such opinions, recommendations, and advice as may conduce to an amicable arrangement according to the best judgment which the mediatory Power may form. There is, therefore, nothing in our position of neutrality which should prevent advice being given, either to the Allies or to Austria, to accept any proposals which the British Government might at the request of the one party transmit to the other; and if it be thought, as seems pretty clear, that a continuation of the war would lead to a state of things in which Austria would not get conditions of peace as little disadvantageous as those which have now been offered, it would be a friendly office towards Austria, and in no degree whatever inconsistent with the character of neutrality, to advise Austria to accept those conditions.

'But, moreover, it seems generally admitted that to the treaty of peace which is to conclude this war, and to the arrangements of that treaty, Great Britain with other Powers, not parties to the war, ought to be parties. But Great Britain cannot be party to a treaty simply to register arrangements made by other Powers. If Great Britain is to be a party to a treaty, the British Crown and Government must be a party to the negotiations by which that treaty is to be settled, and must approve of the arrangements which such treaty is to sanction ; and it is therefore perfectly in accordance with the double character in which we stand, as neutral in the war and of future party to the treaty of peace, that we should express an opinion as to any proposals tending to establish a basis on which negotiations for peace should be founded; and the more especially when invited by the proposing party to do so. The present position, however, of the belligerents, I admit, does not encourage expectation of an immediate arrangement. The Emperor of the French cannot depart from his declaration that Italy must be free to the Adriatic, and, on the other hand, the Emperor of Austria may find it difficult to abandon a strong position taken up by an unbroken though defeated army, to evacuate fortresses not yet attacked, and to relinquish a province of which he still holds possession; and he may think that the erection of that province into an independent separate State, even under a member of his family, would not be sufficient satisfaction. To overcome his reluctance by setting before him the probable results of continued hostilities would be a friendly office, and may not be altogether a hopeless one. It may be mortifying to Austria to make willingly the concessions required of her, but would it be more for her advantage to sustain further defeats and larger military losses, and to have her inability successfully to resist her antagonists shown to the utmost extent? ... If Austria were to consent to the conditions now offered her, she might retain that connection with Venetia which the placing an Austrian Archduke as its ruler would give.'

In August, 1859, he wrote: 'We should incur a heavy responsibility, from which we should be unable to relieve ourselves, if force should be used to coerce the people of Italian States to take back their former dynasties, and it could be alleged that the British Government, foreseeing that such employment of force was possible, had not employed the moral influence of Great Britain to prevent it by a timely remonstrance and protest. The real question at issue is, whether a nation belongs to its ruler, or whether the ruler belongs to the nation? The first position is maintained by the despotic sovereigns of Europe, and was the doctrine of the House of Stuart and their adherents; the latter position the foundation on which the Houses of Great Britain, of France, and of Belgium rest. And with regard to any reversionary rights which Austria may claim upon those duchies, if it be admitted that the people of those States are entitled to set aside the existing dynasties on account of their participation with Austria in hostilities against Italian freedom, they must surely be equally entitled to set aside the contingent and reversionary rights of Austria herself. When the British nation declared the abdication of James II and called William III to the throne, they set aside not only the existing rights of James, but also the contingent and reversionary rights of any persons who might claim through him. It seems very difficult to foretell how the Italian complication will be cleared up, but the hasty and vaguely worded agreements of Villafranca appear to contain the seeds of much difficulty and conflict of opinion'—sound doctrine, not quite recognised by many in England at that time, when they wished to back the *pouvoir légitime* of the Austrian Archdukes in Parma, Tuscany, and Modena.

He again writes a little later: 'The intervention [in Italian affairs] which all parties agreed that their country ought to abstain from, was active interference by force of arms in the war then going on [between France and Austria], but neither of the great political parties meant or asserted that this country should not interfere by its advice and opinions in regard to the matters to which the war related. Neither I nor any of those who acted with me ever contemplated giving any other meaning to the doctrine of non intervention, and that such a meaning was never attached to it by the Conservative leaders while they were in office is proved from one end of the recently published Blue Book to the other. The whole course of the Derby Government in regard to the matters on which the war turned was one uninterrupted series of interventions by advice, by opinions, and by censure, now addressed to one party, now to another. Whatever may be thought of the judgment shown by them, or of the bias by which they were guided, the principle on which they acted was undoubtedly right and proper. England is one of the greatest Powers of the world. No event or series of events bearing on the balance of power or on possibilities of peace or war, can be matters of indifference to her, and her right to have and to express opinions on matters thus bearing on her interests is unquestionable and she is equally entitled to give upon such matters any advice which she may think useful, or to suggest any arrangements which she may deem conducive to the general good. There is no doubt that the Conservative party since they have ceased to be responsible for the conduct of affairs have held a different doctrine, and in their anxiety lest the influence of England should be exerted for the benefit of Italy, and to the disadvantage of Austria, have contended that any participation by Great Britain in the negotiations for the settlement of Italy would be a departure from the principle of non-intervention, but their own practice while in office refutes their newly adopted doctrine in opposition; and if that doctrine were to be admitted, Great Britain would by her own act reduce herself to the rank of a third-class European State.'

In December, 1859, he remarks: 'I have argued, and I think conclusively, that the principle once admitted that no force shall be used to coerce the people of Central Italy, the measure of annexation to Piedmont ought to follow as a necessary consequence, provided that the people of Central Italy continue to desire that union, for it would be a mere play upon words to say that no compulsion shall be put upon the people of Central

Italy directly, but that indirectly and through the Sardinian Government threatened with force, compulsion shall be put upon them to prevent them from obtaining what they desire to have. The policy which we are urging in regard to Italy is precisely the same in principle as that which I laboriously, perseveringly, and successfully acted upon throughout the long negotiations upon the affairs or Belgium. There was then in this country a Dutch party, as there is now an Austrian party, desirous of compelling a people to submit again to a domination which had been irksome, and which they had shaken off. But there is this difference between the two cases, that the Dutch party was numerous, whereas we may depend upon it the Austrian party, as regards the re-subjection of Italy to the Austrian yoke, is extremely small, and in no respect represents the public feeling of this country. I have said that Piedmont even with the addition of Central Italy will have to lean on Italy for support, though it would not have so often to apply for aid as if it were a smaller or weaker State. This statement was well founded, and was intended to meet the objections which some persons about the Emperor are understood to have made to the union, namely, that Piedmont, so enlarged, would become hostile, or at least dangerous, as a neighbour to France. It is self-evident that the more Piedmont is strengthened by enlargement, the less dependent on France she will be; but it is also clear that enlarged as she may be, she must always, from geographical contiguity with the larger Power, France, and also in contact with a hostile neighbour in Austria, be obliged to look to France for support. With regard to the annexation of Central Italy to Piedmont, the Prussian Government take a similar view of that matter, and are of opinion that, if the Archdukes cannot be restored (and it is impossible now to suppose that they can be), the annexation of Central Italy to Piedmont would be a much better arrangement than the creation of a separate State. The affairs of Italy, its pacification, and the best mode of assuring its internal and external independence, are the main and almost the only objects for which the Congress is invited to meet.'

In May, 1860, he thus sums up the general position in Europe:

'The events of the last few months have made a great and serious change in the aspect of European affairs, and in the prospect of European tranquillity. From the time when the present Emperor of the French ascended the throne of France till the conclusion of the recent Italian wars, the policy of the French Government seemed to be founded on an abnegation of foreign conquest and territorial aggrandisement, and upon friendly alliance with Great Britain. These two principles of French policy were indeed so far inseparably connected that alliance between England and France can exist only so long as the policy of France is not directed to territorial aggrandisement. During the above-mentioned period, notwithstanding some of those occasional differences of opinion which must inevitably from time to time arise between the Governments of two great nations having frequently divergent interests in various parts of the world, her Majesty's Government had no reason materially to complain of the Government of France. When the aggression of Russia upon the Turkish Empire called for measures of repression on the part of those Powers of Europe who are more especially interested in preventing the dismemberment of the Ottoman Empire, and that derangement of the balance of power which would arise from the annexation of portions of the Turkish Empire to any already powerful State, the Emperor of the French loyally co-operated with us.

'The French Emperor, indeed, at that time appeared to be so far from animated by a systematically warlike policy, that he was more anxious for an early termination of the war than was the British Government, and in the course of our negotiations for peace our Government found that the Emperor was disposed to make peace upon terms which we thought too easy for the enemy. In the same manner the French Emperor readily concurred with us in concluding a treaty with the King of Sweden for securing against Russian aggression some important naval stations on the northern coast of Norway. Soon after the conclusion of the Russian war the Sepoy mutiny in India broke out, and the Emperor offered us every facility for the passage of our troops through France, and tendered his good offices with the Pacha of Egypt to obtain permission for their passage through Egypt in order to hasten the arrival in India of reinforcements we were sending thither.

'In the beginning of 1859 the Emperor for the first time, by a speech which he made on January 1, gave indications of an intention to disturb by warlike preparations the tranquillity of Europe. The war which soon after broke out in Northern Italy between Austria on the one side, France and Sardinia on the other, had indeed for its immediate cause the invasion of Piedmont by the Austrian army; but it is undeniable that both the belligerent parties had for some time previously contemplated a rupture, and had been making active preparations for such a contingency. The Emperor Napoleon, however, professed by his public declarations that he entered into that war in the most disinterested spirit to rescue Italy from foreign domination, and to restore Italy to the Italians. These declarations obtained for the French arms the sympathy of that large portion of the people of Europe who took an interest in the welfare of Italy. But at length it came out that from the commencement of that war the Emperor had begun a new system of policy, and that, notwithstanding his declarations of disinterestedness and boast that he had made war only for an idea, he had made arrangements binding on Sardinia, by which the probable result of the war, namely, a considerable accession of territory for Sardinia, should be deemed a reason for an important acquisition of territory by France.

'This contemplated arrangement has since been carried into effect, and as the price of the incorporation of Tuscany and Romagna into the kingdom of Sardinia, the county of Nice and the whole of Savoy have been added to the French Empire. Endeavours have been made to induce the French to give to the Swiss Confederation some adequate security against the danger to its independence which must arise from the French occupation of Savoy, but in vain. This security could not be given except by the cession to Switzerland of the southern shore of the Lake of Geneva, and of a good military line on the frontier of the Valais. In the meantime, reports in Europe abound of a variety of schemes of French territorial aggrandisement. It is said that Ortega, before his execution, declared that he had been encouraged in his enterprise by the Emperor, and it is alleged that the Emperor had agreed with Count Montemolin that, if the Carlist attempt had succeeded, the price of the acknowledgment and support of France was to have been an advance of the French frontier from the Pyrenees to the Ebro, or that the Balearic Islands should be ceded to France. It is said that Marshal O'Donnel twice stated to the Morocco plenipotentiaries that the French in Algeria will make an attack on Morocco. The

Emperor is reported to have said that it was necessary for France to have the Palatinate, and to acquire Saarbrück and Saar, part of the Rhenish territory of Prussia. It is reported that there is impatience to get rid of the pending questions in Italy, because the French Government desires to turn its attention to Turkey.

'These reports may be incorrect, but they have their foundation in the general opinion of Europe that the Emperor has adopted a policy of aggrandisement. And the French Government, convinced, as all sane men must be, that no Power in the world has the slightest intention of attacking France, had reduced its army and navy to a moderate peace establishment, less credit would be given to these reports; but, on the contrary, no doubt can be entertained that the French army arrangements are so organised that a force of 600,000 men might be placed under arms within the short period of a month, while great and incessant exertions are making to place the French navy upon the most efficient footing. In short, the French establishments are rapidly assuming such a condition as cannot be required for peace. M. Lafitte, the great Paris banker, was in England during the Epsom races, and held language hostile and insulting to England. He said that England wished to thwart and control France, but is powerless and unable to do so; that France is determined to have the left bank of the Rhine, and to annex Belgium, and will do so notwithstanding the ill-will of England. In the meantime the diplomatic action of France is directed towards separating the Great Powers from each other, and winning over to her views one Power after the other by offers of arrangements suited to the separate interests of each, on condition that each should connive at or concur in some scheme of territorial aggrandisement.

'It is by a full and frank communication between the Powers, and by a common policy for common objects, that the best chance will be afforded of defeating these schemes. I think it desirable to enter into confidential communication with Austria and Prussia, to propose to them that each of the three Powers—Britain, Austria, and Prussia—should make known to each other any overture they may receive from France tending to any change of the existing state of territorial possession in Europe, and that no answer should he given to such proposal until the Government to which it has been made shall have had an answer from the other two. This should not be an agreement for joint action … The policy of Great Britain, subject to exception in special cases, is to keep free from prospective engagements, and to deal with events when they happen according to the circumstances of the moment. In the meanwhile, it is incumbent on the British nation to collect its strength, to place its military and naval establishments in the most efficient state of organisation, and to secure the means of rapid augmentation if at any time the course of events should render augmentation indispensable. The salutary and restraining action of a great Power like England is not confined to the employment of physical force. If it is known to be strong within itself, and capable of exertion when required, its diplomatic action will command attention, and will often powerfully influence the course of events, and by dealing timely with beginnings may prevent proceedings which, if unchecked, would lead to great and disastrous international convulsions.'

The fortification scheme adopted for Portsmouth and other places was an outcome of the fears mentioned in this note.

On the cession of Savoy to France, relations became somewhat strained between England and France. In 1860 Lord Palmerston writes:

'Count de Flahault came to me just as I was going down to the House, wishing to have some talk before he went to Paris; and I, unable to wait, took the Count down in my brougham to the House. Count Flahault said he should see the Emperor, and wished to know what he might say to him as from Lord Palmerston. I said I could only refer Count Flahault to what Lord John Russell had said in the House of Commons. Count Flahault hoped not, as what had been then said was personally offensive to the Emperor. I did not see in what way it could be so considered. Count Flahault said that Lord Grey had expressed distrust, but admitted that no objection could be taken to the latter part of his speech as to the political course which England might follow. I said distrust may be founded on either or both of two grounds—either upon the supposition of intentional deceit, or upon such frequent changes of purpose and of conduct as to show that no reliance can be placed upon the continuance of the intentions or policy of the moment, and Count Flahault must admit that, without imputing the first, there is ample ground for a feeling founded on the second consideration. Count Flahault said his great object was to prevent war between the two countries. I said that I feared the Emperor and Thouvenel had schemes and views which tended to bring about that result, and might array Europe against France. Count Flahault did not fear that, but was apprehensive that irritation on both sides might bring on war between England and France. I said that I was most anxious to prevent such a war, but, if it was forced upon England, England would fearlessly accept it, whether in conjunction with a confederated alliance or singly and by herself, that the nation would rise and rally as one man, and that though, speaking to a Frenchman, I ought perhaps not to say so, yet I could not refrain from observing that the examples of history led me to conclude that the result of a conflict between English and French upon anything like equal terms would not be unsatisfactory to us. Count Flahault said that he had been in the Battle of Waterloo, and knew what English troops were, but that the French army now is far superior to that which fought on that day. I said no doubt it was, and so is the present English army; but with regard to the excellence of the French army I would remind Count Flahault of what passed between Marshal Tallard and the Duke of Marlborough when the former was taken prisoner at the Battle of Blenheim "*Vous venez, Milord,*" said the Marshal, "*de battre les meilleures troupes de l'Europe.*" "*Exceptez toujours,*" replied Marlborough, "*celles qui les ont battues.*" "But," said the Count, "what I fear is an invasion of this country, for which steam affords such facilities, and which would be so disastrous to England." I replied that steam tells both ways, for defence as well as for attack; and that, as for invasion, though it would no doubt be a temporary evil, we were under no apprehension as to its results; that a war between England and France would doubtless be disastrous to both countries, but it is by no means certain which of the two would suffer the most. Arrived at the House, we took leave of each other, Count Flahault saying he should not say anything to the Emperor calculated to increase the irritation which he expected to find, but should endeavour to exercise a calming influence. I said that of course the Count would judge for himself what he should say, but that the Count must have observed what was the state of public feeling and opinion in this country. The conversation was carried on in the most friendly manner.'

During the last Ministry of Lord Palmerston political parties were undergoing changes. The old order was changing, and changing much faster than he ever realised. Only two years after his death there came—in the shape of a Reform Bill passed by a Tory Administration—what he would probably have considered the political deluge. We have frequently had occasion to note, that with parliamentary reform as advocated by such leaders as Bright and Cobden, Palmerston never had the slightest sympathy. Continental politics were changing also. The inevitable conflict between Germany and France, the annihilation of the Second Empire, the consolidation of the German Empire, the unification of Italy, and the far-reaching consequences necessarily following all these great movements, were rapidly taking form. In his own Cabinet one of his colleagues was beginning to make it evident to all that the next Liberal Premier would be of very different stamp from the man whose own statement as that he had not faction enough in him to fit him for Opposition—a saying which lent itself in some small degree to the perverted view that he had no principles which he considered worthy of eager support. His closing years were thus in some measure a season of pause. The Conservatives, afraid of what the development under any possible successor might be, were not eager to dis-place him. The Liberal party was slowly but surely reaching that parting of the ways which may be said to divide the party of evolution and adapta-tion from that which favours theory at the expense of experience. To some extent Palmerston was conscious of this, and on one occasion remarked to Lord Shaftesbury, 'Gladstone will soon have it all his own way; and whenever he gets my place, we shall have strange doings.'

The old veteran, however, was allowed to pass away in peace. In 1861 he became Warden of the Cinque Ports, and whilst he was passing through the picturesque and old-fashioned forms of his installation, the opening events of the great Civil War in the United States were taking place.

Unlike Mr Gladstone, who declared that Mr Jefferson Davis had 'made a nation' when the States of the Southern Confederacy were at death grip with the Northern United States Government, Lord Palmerston said in 1861: 'As to North America, our best and true policy seems to be to go on as we have begun, and to keep quite clear of the conflict between North and South. It is true that there have been cases in Europe in which allied Powers have said to fighting parties, like the man in "The Critic," "in the Queen's name I bid you drop your swords;" but those cases are rare and peculiar; the love of quarrelling and of fighting is inherent in man, and to prevent its indulgence is to impose restraints on natural liberty. A State may so shackle its own subjects; but it is an infringement on national independence to restrain other nations. The only excuse would be the danger to the interfering parties if the conflict went on; but in the American case this cannot be pleaded by the Powers of Europe. The want of cotton would not justify such a proceeding, unless, indeed, the distress created by that want was far more serious than it is likely to be. The only thing to do seems to be to lie on our oars and to give no pretext to the Washingtonians to quarrel with us, while, on the other hand, we maintain our rights and those of our fellow-countrymen.'

These had to be vindicated during the same year when the Commissioners of the Southern Confederacy were arrested on board the 'Trent,' a British steamer, by United States officers. One of the last acts of the Prince Consort, whose death Lord Palmerston deplored in private as well as in public, was to soften the expressions of a despatch remonstrating with the United States Government on this subject, lest unnecessary offence might be given to the Northern Americans when they had much to make them sore. The Guards and other troops were sent to Canada, and through the Prince's counsel the request made to the Americans for explanation was so couched, that a conciliatory conduct was adopted, and the threatened war with our brethren across the sea averted.

The death of the Prince,

The shadow of whose loss
Commingled with the gloom
Of imminent war, moved like eclipse

across our country, and the anxieties of the time, aggravated a bad fit of gout by which Lord Palmerston was attacked, and his handwriting was never afterwards as firm and bold as it had been in former years.

A letter of this period to Mr Gladstone, which is quoted by Mr Ashley, refers to Mr Gladstone's demand in speeches delivered at Manchester for increased economy:

'Increased commercial intercourse may add to the links of mutual interest between us and the French; but commercial interest is a link that snaps under the pressure of national passions. Witness the bitter enmity to England lately freely vented, and now with difficulty suppressed, by those Northern States of America with whom we have the most extensive commercial intercourse. Well, then, at the head of this neighbouring nation, who would like nothing so well as a retaliatory blow upon England, we see an able, active, wary, counsel-keeping, but ever-planning sovereign; and we see this sovereign organising an army, which, including his reserve, is more than six times greater in amount than the whole of our regular forces in our two islands; and at the same time labouring hard to create a navy equal to, if not superior to, ours. Give him a cause of quarrel, which any foreign Power may at any time invent or create if so minded— give him the command of the Channel, which permanent or accidental naval superiority might afford him—and then calculate if you can (for it would pass my reckoning power to do so) the disastrous consequences to the British nation which a landing of an army of from one to two hundred thousand men would bring with it. Surely even a large yearly expenditure for army and navy is an economical insurance against such a catastrophe.'

The Conservatives were especially amused and delighted with the manner in which Palmerston repressed the 'advanced wing' of his own party, especially when they described the millennium as having already arrived, and sought to persuade their country to turn all its swords into ploughshares. When Cobden opposed the increase to the votes on fortifications, and declared that, as for fears of French invasion, 'Why, the labourers on the farms in Sussex alone could throw up fortifications sufficient in a week to stop a French army,' Lord Palmerston rose, and, with a somewhat confused recollection of available classical quotations, but with a very precise sense of the value of Cobden's advice on such an occasion, said: 'The hon. gentleman talks of the Sussex labourers throwing up defences that would stop a French army. The hon. gentleman had best stick to—his—his— ahem—"crepidam."' And much the House laughed at this way of putting the good advice, 'Cobbler Cobden, stick to your last.'

On the proposal of the French Emperor that we should work with him in regard to the action of Prussia in agreeing with the Government of St Petersburg to support a Polish rising, Lord Palmerston wrote (1863) to King Leopold of Belgium: 'Your Majesty will have learnt that we declined to fall into the trap which the Emperor of the French laid for us by his scheme for a violent identical Note to be presented to Prussia. It was evidently intended that the demands of such a Note being refused, or evaded, a pretence would thereby have been afforded to France for an occupation of the Prussian Rhenish Provinces, and the French Government has shown much ill humour at the failure of the scheme. But the danger to Prussia and other States is not over. If the Polish revolution goes on, and Prussia is led to take an active part in any way against the Poles, the Emperor of the French is sure sooner or later, upon some pretext, to enter the Rhenish Provinces as a means of coercing Prussia to be neutral. Your Majesty would render an essential service to Prussia and to Europe if you could exert your influence with the King of Prussia to abstain from any action of any kind whatever beyond the frontiers of his own territory.'

Roebuck in the House of Commons entered into an account of his communications with the Emperor of the French on the subject of the French navigation laws and about American affairs. Lord Palmerston, in July 1863, expressed his hope that this might be the last time that any member of Parliament should bring to the British Parliament a message from a foreign sovereign, or relate to Parliament any conversation he had had with any foreign sovereign.

In 1863 occurred the recrudescence of the dispute between the Danes and Germans in reference to Schleswig-Holstein, which ended in the annexation of the whole country by Germany. I remember a dinner at which a lady much inclined to 'pump' Ministers on politics was seated between Lord Palmerston and me. She opened fire on Lord Palmerston on this question of the Duchies, and I heard him say, 'Well, I had that matter once at my fingers' ends, but, upon my word, I have quite forgotten all its complications.' He never liked to 'become expansive' on public topics in private society, although to his own correspondents among the ladies he opened his mind freely enough on political subjects.

In 1864 he thus sums up his views of the situation: 'It is not unlikely that Austria and Prussia, reckoning upon our passive attitude, contemplate the occupation of Copenhagen, and think to imitate what the first Napoleon did at Vienna and Berlin, and mean to dictate at the Danish capital their own terms of peace. We should be laughed at if we stood by and allowed this to be done.' To Lord J. Russell he wrote: 'I wrote this morning to Apponyi [Austrian Ambassador], asking him to come to me to give me half an hour's conversation. He came accordingly. I said I wished to have some friendly and unreserved conversation with him, not as between an English Minister and the Austrian Ambassador, but as between Palmerston and Apponyi; that what I was going to say related to serious matters, but I begged that nothing I might say should be looked upon as a threat, but only as a frank explanation between friends on matters which might lead to disagreements, and with regard to which, unless timely explanations were given as to possible consequences of certain things, a reproach might afterwards be made that timely explanation might have diverted disagreeable results. I said that we have from the beginning taken a deep interest in favour of Denmark, not from family ties, which have little influence on English policy, and sometimes act unfavourably, but, first, that we have thought from the beginning that Denmark has been harshly and unjustly treated; and, secondly, we deem the integrity and independence of the State which commands the entrance to the Baltic objects of interest, to England. That we abstained from taking the field in defence of Denmark for many reasons—from the season of the year—from the smallness of our army—and the great risk of failure in a struggle with all Germany by land. That with regard to operations by sea the positions would be reversed : we are strong, Germany is weak; and the German ports in the Baltic, North Sea, and Adriatic would be greatly at our command. Speaking for myself personally, and for nobody else, I must frankly tell him, that if an Austrian squadron were to pass along our coasts and ports and go into the Baltic to help in any way against Denmark, I should look upon it as an affront and insult to England. That I could not and would not stand such a thing; and that, unless in such a case a superior British squadron were to follow, with such orders for acting as the case might require, I would not continue to hold my present position: and such a case would probably lead to collision—that is, war; and in my opinion Germany and especially Austria would be the sufferer in such a war. I should deeply regret such a result, because it is the wish of England to be well with Austria; but I am confident that I should be borne out by public opinion. I again begged that he would not consider this communication as a threat, but simply as a friendly reminder of consequences which might follow a possible course of action.'

In 1865 there was another general election, and Lord Palmerston was again elected, and for the last time, MP for Tiverton; but his health was failing, and in October the mournful news spread that he had died at Brocket—in harness to the last. I well remember how his grandson, Lord Jocelyn, then with me at Trinity, Cambridge, brought me the first news, and how every student in the streets and halls that day spoke sadly of the event, and we all felt that a type of some of the best qualities in English manhood had been lost to our country. Mr Ashley says that he was himself a witness of an incident of the last weeks of Lord Palmerston's life, which he thought most characteristic of the man: 'There were some high railings immediately opposite the front door, and Lord Palmerston, coming out of the house without his hat, went straight up to them after casting a look all round to see that no one was looking. He then climbed deliberately over the top rail down to the ground on the other side, turned round, climbed back again, and then went indoors. It was clear that he had come out to test his strength, and to find out for himself in a practical way how far he was gaining or losing ground. Not that he had any excessive dread of death, for, as he put it one day in homely fashion to his doctor, when pressing for a frank opinion as to his state, "When a man's time is up, there is no use in repining."'

On the sad day when all that was great and distinguished in England met in the old historical Abbey on the banks of the Thames to pay a last mark of respect to the statesman who had gone from us, in the midst of gloom, moral and physical, a gleam of sunshine appeared at the very moment when his body was being lowered to its last abode, and the prevailing darkness was for a time dispelled. That slight, that accidental coincidence, gave rise to a beautiful expression from a great and eloquent clergyman, who said that 'when human minds gifted beyond their fellows quitted this world, they left something of light behind them; and at this moment I believe there is not one of us, whatever may be our powers, whatever our opportunities, who will wish to go away without determining to follow that bright example.'

XII

Some Personal Characteristics of Lord Palmerston

MANY OF THE MIDDLE-AGED among us can still recollect the man of whom Sir Robert Peel, an antagonist, said in 1848, immediately after he had delivered his oft-quoted speech in the 'Don Pacifico' debate, 'We are all proud of him.' We can recollect the fretting occasioned among the Liberals by his so-called 'high-handed' way of dealing with foreign Powers, and the fear they had of him as one who dreaded not war. We can remember the curiosity with which Tories regarded him, as one who could act with their opponents and yet was so much one of themselves in desiring that Britain should not lose her influence as a Power in the world. We heard of his popularity as a thorough Englishman, who loved sport, spoke and acted straightly, 'gave back as good as he got in debate, and who used to be called 'the evergreen Premier.'

Some of us may have more personal reminiscences to tell, and may have seen him rise quickly and lightly, when near fourscore, from his seat in the House of Commons, and speak with clearness and directness, but with no attempt at eloquence, and often with some hesitation, at the table; his black frock-coat buttoned across the well-knit and erect figure of middle stature, his sentences spoken towards the bar of the House; his grey short hair brushed forward, and the grey whiskers framing the head, erect on the shoulders. Some may remember, under the shaven chin, the loose bow-knot, neatly tied, at the throat, the bit of open shirt-front with short standing collars. Some may have seen that same figure standing unwearied at the low brass railing that encircles the space which is devoted to Privy Councillors in front of the Throne in the House of Lords, or, if they were admitted there as youths connected with the Peers, may have stood beside the veteran political leader as he listened to the discussion proceeding in the 'gilded chamber,' and may have looked up at that refined and resolute face, and, with the irreverence of youth, have noticed that the whiskers were much greyer close to the cheek, and that the darker hue that pervaded them was not the result either of old age or of early nature. Some may have attended his last receptions at Cambridge House, that handsome white building standing a little retired from Piccadilly, to which its court opens by two wide entrances. There they may have been charmed with the old-fashioned and frank courtesy that bade them welcome as soon as they had reached the centre room at the stair top, which was the place at which the firm figure of the old statesman, clad in well-made evening dress and very neat polished boots, met them and gave them a hearty shake of the hand, as they passed on to be greeted with equal courtesy by Lady Palmerston. But age was telling in those days even on her husband, and he used to forget whom he had greeted, and repeat the kindly hand-shake twice or even thrice.

One of the last of the great receptions was given in honour of General Garibaldi. This was a sore subject with most of the Conservatives, who could not bear that the red shirted patriot and revolutionary soldier should be courted and caressed. He, more than any other, had made Italy a nation under one monarch, and had shown himself favourable to the House of Savoy. But that he had caused the King of Naples to fly, and had attacked the Pope as an earthly sovereign, was sufficient to make good Tories shake their heads. Was it possible, they asked, that the Duchess of Sutherland was to receive him at Stafford House? And when he came accompanied by the shouting myriads of London who gave him such a reception as they had given to no foreign crowned head, it was said that in the Cabinet the result of Garibaldi's visit on public feeling was questioned, and that one member said, 'What shall we do with Garibaldi?' 'Do?' said Lord Palmerston; 'oh, let's marry him to the rich Miss ——' 'But he has a wife already,' was the rejoinder. 'Oh, then,' said Palmerston, 'we'll get —— ' (mentioning an eminent colleague) 'to explain her away!'

It was during these days that he astonished everyone by his wonderful spirits, and by the physical power shown by him. He thought nothing of riding down to Harrow for a speech day, and the 'boys' of that time remember how lightly he dismounted from his horse and came into the Hall, arranging his hair with a little pocket-comb he carried. Then after the speeches were over there was a holiday asked for, and the head-master, conscientious and strict, felt bound to declare that two days had already been given, and that he felt much difficulty in granting a third. 'Oh, I remember,' said the Prime Minister, 'that Price in his book on the Picturesque lays it down as a canon in painting that you should never only have two objects of prominence in a picture, that there should always be a third. Don't you think the principle may be applied here, and that two days only would not present a perfect picture?' What he was as a boy he remained to his life's end strong in body and robust in mind; led by no fantastic genius, but by the good light of fair judgment.

No one ever had a better appetite either for food or for work. It was remarked that often at dinner he never let a dish pass without taking some of it. So it was in 'affairs'—which word generally denotes with us our business as citizens rather than our own. He never let any public event, or incidents leading to events, pass without sounding to the best of his ability the depth of public feeling which was around him, and the set of the currents he experienced. But, unlike some men, he had no idea of being carried helplessly along on any current, however strong, which might lead him whither he would not. He formed his opinions, and he held fast to them. The energy of his character was not called out to defend surrender to that which he had denounced, nor was it enlisted to further that which he had called wrong. He was a leader led by his own honest thoughts of what was best for his country. He never could be called a leader who might be reckoned on to lead wheresoever the majority of his followers told him he must go. He could never capitulate to a despotic power, whether that were exercised under the guise of religion, or held its sway under the travesty of freedom, nationality, or justice. He put aside the sham, and worked for the cause of constitutional liberty wherever he recognised it, though it might not be the power to lift him to office. 'I will not be dragged through the dirt,' he exclaimed on one occasion when urged to acquiesce in what his conscience disapproved.

Nor with all his hard-headed common sense was he unconcerned when he saw the troubles of others, nor were his affections and his sympathies the less keen because he 'would stand no nonsense.' He laboured assiduously, sparing neither time nor expense, to help his Irish tenants and cottiers during their day of difficulty, assisting those who desired to go to America to find comparative wealth there, and lavishly aiding those who remained to step out on paths that might lead them to better conditions at home. In the circle of his own family there was nothing, even when he was most busy, that escaped his affectionate care, and to the time of his death he and his house were the beloved centre of a large array of kinsfolk.

Sir Augustus Clifford said of Lord Palmerston's boyhood that he was reckoned the best-tempered and most plucky boy at Harrow, as well as a young man of great promise. 'I can remember Temple fighting "behind school" a great boy called Salisbury, twice his size, and he would not give in, but was brought home with black eyes and a bloody nose.'

His appearance in 1837 is thus described: 'In person Lord Palmerston is tall and handsome. His face is round and of the darkest hue. His hair is black, and always exhibits proofs of the skill and attention of the *friseur*. His clothes are in the extreme of fashion. He is very vain of his personal appearance.'

Sir William Fraser sketches him as he appeared to a later generation: 'Lord Palmerston on horseback looked a big man, and standing at the table of the House he did not appear ill-proportioned. Each foot, to describe it mathematically, was a "four-sided irregular figure." His portraits in *Punch* are very like him. Those with a flower or straw in the mouth are the best. He had a very horsey look.'

Through the 'Greville Memoirs' we get two or three glimpses of him as he appeared to that none too kindly observer: 'Palmerston is beaten in Hants, at which everybody rejoices, for he is marvellously unpopular; they would have liked to illuminate the Foreign Office. The other night I met some clerks in the Foreign Office to whom the very name of Palmerston is hateful, but I was surprised to hear them … give ample testimony to his abilities. They said that he wrote admirably, and could express himself perfectly in French, very sufficiently in Italian, and understood German; that his diligence and attention were unwearied—he read everything, and wrote an immense quantity; that the foreign Ministers (who detest him) did him justice as an excellent man of business. His great fault is want of punctuality, and never caring for an engagement if it did not suit him, keeping everybody waiting for hours on his pleasure or caprice. This testimony is beyond suspicion, and it is confirmed by the opinions of his colleagues; but it is certain that he cut a very poor figure in Parliament all the time he was in office before.'

The views entertained by the clerks and subordinates about their chief may have been coloured by the fact that he much objected to anything 'slipshod,' whether in expression or in orthography. It is remarkable how he never hesitated to repeat the same word over and over again in a sentence if additional clearness of meaning could thereby be given. He wrote an uncommonly good hand, and was always very intolerant of anyone less blessed with that description of manual skill. The secretaries at home and abroad 'caught it hot' when a badly written despatch came into his hands. The scathing memoranda which he penned for the benefit of the delinquent were written, as one of his old subordinates says, 'on a half sheet of note-paper, with a reference carefully made in the left-hand corner to the despatch remarked upon, inserted by him into it, and returned in it to the department, and afterwards sent by the latter in original to the embassy or legation concerned with the next batch of despatches. I recollect having received a memorandum in 1851 when the others in the chancellerie were all on leave. I won't vouch for the exact words, but it was, as far as I in the following terms: "Tell the gentleman who copied this despatch to write a larger, rounder hand, to join on the letters in the words, and to use blacker ink." You will recollect that "blacker ink" was the refrain of most of his memoranda, and that it made us think he was going blind. But it was not handwriting alone, but likewise on spelling and construction that "Palmy" kept a sharp look-out. I remember at Berlin an amusing memo, sent to our legation. Our *Chargé d'Affaires* at the time had occasion to use the word battalions, and inadvertently spelt it with one "t" and two "l's," "batallions," instead of "battalions." This brought down the following remark: "Tell A. B. to direct his amanuensis to place his battalions on the English and not on the French footing." The attaché who had made the copy was very indignant, and said that Lord Palmerston had himself used an expression, "amanuensis," which was not English, and, moreover, that his (the attaché's) duty was only to copy. In another case, where the letter had, as the writer thought, been most clearly expressed, but had repeated after a parenthesis a "that" which had already been placed before the parenthesis, Lord Palmerston observed, "Tell —— to strike out his redundant 'that.'" The writer was much annoyed at what he called this freedom, but I afterwards had frequently to remonstrate with him because he would always strike out "thats" which were necessary to make the sense quite clear.'

Sir William Fraser, to whom reference has already been made above, has left on record some reminiscences which deserve a place here: 'Lord Palmerston presided at an annual dinner of the Royal Literary Fund. I asked Monckton Milnes, afterwards Lord Houghton, how Palmerston got on at the dinner; he answered, "For a man who never read a book in his life, I think he did very well." Lord Palmerston might have led the House of Commons at thirty-five; but declined: giving as his reason that "his life would be a perpetual canvass," and that he could not endure it. Whether this were the real cause or not I do not know; the reason of his ultimately achieving his position in Parliament was that he was twenty years older than any other leading man: that he knew the country well: and that on one subject he knew a great deal, and no one else knew anything: foreign affairs.

'Lord Palmerston never was a good speaker: he had a hesitation which came in at the most inappropriate times: a good voice, but no art; in speaking he would constantly use an anti-climax: he would say, for instance "The language of the honourable gentleman is unusual, unparliamentary, violent, discreditable, and ahem!"—a pause—"to be deprecated." I never knew him rise to real eloquence, and on one occasion only did I hear him speak with great ability: this was on the Danish question. Everybody who attended to such matters had been completely puzzled by the complicated affairs of Schleswig-Holstein. The clearest heads could make nothing of it, and the vast majority of the House of Commons did not attempt it. Lord Palmerston made a speech admirable in its clearness. I could not have believed it possible that he could make such a speech, solving the difficulties, and presenting the essential points of the question to the appreciation and comprehension of the House. Disraeli, seeing the effect that had been produced, in his reply characterised the speech as "perspicuous, but not satisfactory." It was splendidly perspicuous. I was not in Parliament at the time of the celebrated "Pacifico speech," nor up to this time have I been able to understand by reading it the effect which it produced; but I may say that except on these two occasions Lord Palmerston never made a great speech.

'It is supposed that a laugh is indicative of character and feeling. I never heard a heartier laugh than Lord Palmerston's: very deep down, and musical. He gave you the impression of perfect good-humour.'

Palmerston had very considerable power of repartee, and now and then used very apt and striking language: 'Nothing,' he once remarked, 'can be more deplorable than an inheritance of triumphant wrong.' When Lord Derby's translation of the 'Iliad' was first announced, a guest at Broadlands told Palmerston that he must keep pace with his great rival by translating the 'Aeneid.' 'Stop till I am out of office, and the parallel will be complete.' On another occasion he laughingly quoted the authority of an eminent physician, that continuance in office, with the resulting employment, was good for the health. 'Would not active opposition do as well?' 'No, no; that stirs up the bile and creates acidity. Ask Disraeli if it does not.'

Nothing created acidity in him; he never said or sanctioned an ill-natured remark on anybody. On being told that a clever assailant regretted a personal attack, he said, 'Tell him I am not the least offended, the more particularly because I think I had the best of it.'

When at the Home Office, a deputation came to him from the town of Rugeley asking that its name might be changed. Why was this request made? Because a man named Palmer, a citizen of that town, had been condemned to death, having been found guilty of poisoning with strychnine a number of people. 'The Rugeley case' was known wherever the English language was spoken. The town smelt of poison, thought its unhappy inhabitants. The name must be changed, and Lord Palmerston was invoked for permission. He listened quietly, and then, in his merry, jaunty way, said, 'Well, gentlemen, I am very sorry for you, and the only thing I can do is to suggest that you call your town "Palmerston"—Palmer being the name of the poisoner.

'He was fond of billiards,' writes Hayward, 'and when at Brocket or Broadlands played three games (neither more nor less) before retiring for the night. He was about on a level with those who play a good deal without taking rank as players. His best stroke was the winning hazard, and fortune favoured him as much in this as in the political game. After three or four flukes he would say, "I think I had better not name my stroke." He was never the least put out by losing, although he enjoyed winning, especially if Lady Palmerston was looking on.'

A correspondent who saw a good deal of him says: 'The impression my intercourse with him left on my mind is simple. He left on my recollection the impression of the possessor of a strong character, and intellect with a coarse grain in it, verging sometimes almost on brutality; and of a mind little exercised on subjects of thought beyond the immediate interests of public and private life, little cultivated, and drawing its stores not from reading, but from experience, and long and varied intercourse with men and women—reminding one in that respect of such women as Madame de Lieven, however otherwise masculine.

'An illustration of this habit of mind occurs to me as I write in Lord Palmerston's well-known doctrine on some public occasion that "Men are naturally good," quite unconscious that there was such a widely held theological dogma as that of "original sin." He did not say it controversially, only it did not occur to him that he was contradicting all the Churches. My clearest picture of Lord Palmerston at Cambridge House is as I used to find him in his working room, standing up at his high desk, almost unapproachable from the fortification of office boxes piled around him. At Broadlands one seldom saw him except at meals, at which, so far as I can remember, he did not talk much. I don't think he cared much for conversation, nor shone in it, though he told a good story now and then. There was always a very long waiting for dinners because Lord Palmerston's messenger was sent off at the latest possible moment. The longest and most animated discourse that I remember hearing from him, and I think he had no audience but myself; was one day when he got on the subject of Louis Philippe and the Spanish marriages, and grew very hot upon it. A conversation which took place on a railway platform between Lord Palmerston and Sir Culling Eardley was amusing from the contrast between the two men, though there is little in it. Sir Culling Eardley was trying to persuade the Prime Minister to have a day of public humiliation ordered on account of long-continued rain (or drought), and Lord Palmerston was fighting him off. "Are things really so bad, Sir Culling?" "My lord, I have just come from the country, and the crops are ruined." "Then it's too late, Sir Culling—past praying for." I think it was at the same time, at the end of his last session, and at Brocket, that I remember Lady Palmerston telling me that he had had a letter from the Queen which gratified him very much, thanking him for the admirable letters which he wrote every night from the House of Commons, describing the debates, &c.'

The constancy with which he attended the sittings of the House of Commons was the wonder of more youthful and more restless members. Hour after hour he sat on the Treasury bench, the daylight from the high-placed windows, or the gas-light from the ceiling of the Chamber, when dusk had come, falling on his grey locks, which were always carefully brushed forward in the old fashion. He seemed usually to be absently regarding the lower woodwork of the massive table, whose top was garnished with multitudinous papers and books of reference and an occasional despatch-box—the table at which the three clerks sit below the Speaker's chair—a heavy piece of furniture, which bears the gilt mace, and sees new members sworn at its side, and is so placed that it resembles a great wooden altar at which the officiating priests of the British Constitution are ranged on their seats on either side, so that each, when he harangues the assembly and delivers incantations to support the faith of his followers, stands at this table. The long rows of the oaken benches, whether they were black with members during an interesting debate, or whether they were almost destitute of occupants and showed their green leather coverings to the eyes in the strangers' gallery, witnessed that resolute and watchful, though seemingly dozing figure, seated constantly in its place. During a 'great night' it was curious to see how apparently unmoved and passive he remained during all the phases of the debate, his face in repose, his eyes looking steadily in front of him, often half closed, his frock-coat buttoned neatly across him, his gloves always on his hands, his neat trousers of a light-toned cloth strapped down to his neat boots. Not a turn of the arguments used escaped him, and yet, when at the end he rose to conclude the debate and to reply, it did not follow that he would reply point by point. On the contrary, important points were sometimes avoided, or he would play round them, and, with the jaunty fun and half mocking raillery he knew so well how to use, he would 'pitch into' an opponent, give the salient facts and the chief motives and reasons he had for his action, in plain phrase, strongly worded but not always expressed with fluency, and then he would call upon his friends to vote in some effective passage which combined English common sense with the concise phraseology born of long knowledge and the ring of an undoubted patriotism and honesty of conviction, which told on his party and ensured him the majority he expected.

A remarkable instance of his characteristic assiduity was the resolution with which he in 1855 set himself to master the forms of the House of Commons. He had been until then chiefly a Departmental Minister, and when he found himself at the head of the Cabinet and leader of the House of Commons, he discovered that even his long experience of that body had not made him familiar with many of its usages. Time after time did the summer morning still find him at his post.

Those who doubt his powers of acute analysis should study his speeches on the international questions which have been discussed. He evinced in these debates a grasp of general principle, a perspicacity of reasoning, which the greatest lawyers in the House might have envied, and which in point of power and cogency gave his views a value far beyond those of any of the other lay members.

It was said that he was inclined to treat matters of grave import with levity. Anecdotes about him have been absurdly used to illustrate this. This accusation of levity was especially the keynote of those who desired to disparage him during the last year of the Crimean War. The public, however, very soon discovered that no accusation could be more unjust. The critics could not distinguish between the subject itself and their own views in regard to it; nor could they see that, while the Premier contented himself with launching a witty javelin against assaults he thought worthy of no more solemn refutation, he at the same time thought deeply on topics which he conceived them not qualified to handle.

In Palmerston's views of the service he owed to his Queen and country there was not a tinge of levity. He was eminently a man with an earnest sense of duty; and underneath his gay and insouciant exterior he bore about with him a never-ceasing and conscientious impression of the deep responsibility of his office. He knew all its affairs. Probably no

First Minister ever ruled this country who was better informed from day to day even of the minor details relating to the different departments of the Government.

Mr Ashley mentions that in Lord Palmerston's eightieth year he rode all over the heights to the north of Portsmouth to see the long line of forts he had caused to be constructed there, and quotes a short, purposelike speech delivered at the opening of a new railroad, on the advantages of quick communication by steam, the want of which he could well remember.

'In former times a gentleman asked his friend in London to come down to him in the country, and the friend came with things to last him a fort-night or three weeks, and he took, perhaps, a week on the journey. Now, if a friend meets another in St James's Street and says, "I shall have some good shooting next week; will you come down to me and spend a few days?" The friend says, "Oh, by all means I shall be charmed. What is the nearest station to your house?" "Well," the friend says, "I am not very well off at present in regard to railway communication; the nearest station is sixteen miles from my house, but it is a good road; you will get a nice fly, and you will come very well." Upon which the invited guest says, "Did you say it was Tuesday you asked me for?" "Yes," says the countryman, "and I think you told me that you were free on that day." Upon which the other replies, "I have a very bad memory. Upon my word, I am very sorry, but I have a particular engage-ment on that day. Some other time I shall be happy to come down to you." (Laughter.) Then he offers himself as a visitor to some other friend who has a station within one or two miles of his house. (Cheers and laughter.)'

Mr Ashley says that Lord Palmerston would never give up anything on account of age. 'He used to go out partridge shooting long after his eyesight was too dim to take correct aim, and persevered in his other outdoor pursuits. Twice during this year, starting at nine o'clock and not getting back till two, he rode over from Broadlands to the training stables at Littleton, to see his horses take a gallop in Winchester Racecourse. He rode down in June to the Harrow speeches, and timed himself to trot the distance from his house in Piccadilly to the Head-Master's door, nearly twelve miles, within the hour, and accomplished it.'

Only a few days before his end, when, so far as the aspect of his face could betoken illness, he appeared as ill as a man could be when about and at work, Lady Palmerston at breakfast alluded to the cattle plague, which was then making great havoc in England. He at once remarked that all the symptoms of the disorder were described by Virgil, and repeated to me some eight lines out of the 'Georgics' descriptive of the disease. He then told me a story of a scrape he got into at Harrow for throwing stones, and the excess of laughter, which he was unable to restrain, with which he recalled the incident was the only token that could have betrayed to Lady Palmerston, to spare whom he always sought to conceal his illness, how weak he was.

'If Lord Palmerston,' said one, soon after his death, who knew him well, 'was the type of an Englishman, he was in many, both of its every-day and of its rarer, aspects a model of official life. Nature was lavish to him of many gifts, and it is the lot of few to bring to the public service that strong will, that iron constitution, and that charm of manner which stood him in such stead during more than fifty years of office. But he had other qualities, homelier it is true, but not the less essential to the position which he attained. It has been said that Lord Palmerston's success was due not so much to any surpassing ability, as to a rare combination of ordinary qualities. But the remark, although in some respects true, is superficial. Probably his greatest intellectual peculiarity was the equipoise of his powers, which gave them an air of complete symmetry, and somewhat baffled the estimate of them in detail. He possessed a union of qualities seldom found to exist together in equal excellence. That a man should be really both grave and gay, both witty and earnest, devoted alike to the routine of an office and to the love of sport and of society—in short, that a states-man should be both merry and wise—shocks the pedantry of the public; and the public are so far right that it requires unusual powers to effect the combination; and these Lord Palmerston possessed.'

Mr Lowe (now Viscount Sherbrooke) said at Romsey on July 22, 1876:

'Greatly as we all admired Lord Palmerston's intellectual power, there was one thing in him that I admired even more—his inexhaustible and indomitable industry and perseverance in the discharge of his duties. At eighty years of age Lord Palmerston was by far the most regular attendant in the House of Commons of any of his Ministry. He came at 4 PM and for four nights of every week he stayed if necessary till 2, never stirring from his place, except perhaps for the purpose of taking a cup of tea. There he was always accessible to everybody, always courteous to everybody, friend or opponent; no reverse, no taunt, none of those accidents to which political life is subject, not the weight of years, not the laborious exertions which he felt called on to make, ever ruffled his temper or disturbed his good-humour, nor did he even seem to think it wonderful that at his age he should be able to undergo these labours. I say then that he was not only a great political leader but a great Englishman. When he undertook a duty he did it thoroughly. He never spared himself. He who had the best society in Europe at his command left it all when work was to be done.'

But at the head of a long list of private and public testimonies to Lord Palmerston's character, abilities, and influence stands that which came from the heart of his friend and colleague, Earl Granville:

'Political contests never deadened the feelings of his heart and warmer affections. There is hardly one of us who, even in his busiest hours, has not received from him timely and considerate advice on matters of purely private and personal nature. Well do I remember, at a time when he delighted the House of Commons at the age of nearly eighty years by giving so close an attendance to his parliamentary duties as had never been given before by any leader of the House, at a time when he was fulfilling all the duties of his high office, he found time for weeks daily to write sheets of social and political news to relieve the hours of sickness of a dear young colleague who was sinking under disease in a far and foreign land. It is impossible not to connect these private virtues, these personal qualities, with the public character of this great man. I had the honour of serving under him at the Foreign Office. Lord Palmerston had very high notions of what ought to be the organisation, the discipline of a public office, and both in the Foreign Office and the War Office his name at first was looked on with almost more of fear than love. But when the permanent staff had time to observe his inflexible justice; when they learned how much harder he was on himself than on the meanest clerk in his department; how, almost to a fault, he took all the great and small labour of the office on himself, thus acquiring a power which enabled him to deal in an extraordinary manner with every departmental question, both in Parliament and in negotiating with foreign Ministers—when they saw this, and when, above all, they observed the chivalry with which he threw himself into the defence of the very meanest of his subordinates if he had a right to claim the protection of his chief, the persons employed in his department instead of offering, as I am bound to say they do, a measured attachment to their chief when they think he fulfils with ability and conscientiousness the duties of his office, these men felt for Lord Palmerston more of the devotion, the passionate attachment, which a conquering army feels for its chief, which the Tenth Legion felt for Caesar, or the Old Guard for Napoleon.'

Speaking of his political career, Earl Granville continued:

'If Lord Palmerston had faults, those faults sprang from the overflowing of the great qualities which he possessed, and from the patriotism which influenced every act of his life. Lord Palmerston knew how to make concessions under changing circumstances, as all wise men do. He knew how to move with the spirit of the age; but there were some great principles which he never deserted through life—his passionate attachment to civil and religious liberty all over the world; his opposition to anything like religious persecution or injustice; his horror of oppression and perfect detestation of slavery in all its forms. His great stimulus was the patriotic feeling to which I have alluded, and to this feeling he added an unbounded belief in the destinies of the country to which he belonged, and a wish to place every Englishman collectively and individually on a pinnacle of honour and glory. These were the qualities, together with unwearied industry, accompanied by gifts of a lighter and more graceful, but not less useful, nature which God had bestowed upon him, which extorted even from unfriendly critics terms of admiration of his winning manner and happy temperament, his English solidity mixed with something of Irish vivacity. The same terms of admiration were expressed in regard to his quickness, his great experience, and his natural and national eloquence. These are the causes which induced his great rival, Sir R. Peel, even in a moment of political attack, to admit that Lord Palmerston was the Minister of whom England was proud, and these were some of the causes which, when he was taken away from us at an age which it is given to few men to attain, yet in the full possession of all his faculties, made it appear to the community at large, without distinction of politics or of class, as almost an unexpected, a premature event.'

These lines, which appeared in *Punch* on October 28, express what very large numbers felt with regard to him:

But his heart was his England's, his idol her honour,
Her friend was his friend, and his foe was her foe
Were her mandate despised, or a scowl cast upon her,
How stern his rebuke, or how vengeful his blow!

Her armies were sad, and her banners were tattered,
And lethargy wrought on her strength like a spell;
He came to the front, the enchantment was scattered—
The rest let a reconciled enemy tell.

As true to our welfare, he did his own mission,
When Progress approached him with Wisdom for guide;
He cleared her a path, and with equal division
Bade quack and fanatic alike stand aside.

Two traits of Lord Palmerston's character rendered him conspicuously successful as a great leader of men. He was entirely fearless, and he never deserted a subordinate. He came to his convictions deliberately. His well-balanced mind and temperament had little in it of the impulsive. He thought without excitement or passion, but the conviction once attained, the resolution once taken, he never looked back. He might be swayed by the public voice before his determination was made, but never afterwards. And having himself a strong sense of the responsibility of office, he had sympathy for all under him; and his counsel in difficulty, and support under imputation, were never failing—the only sure way to obtain hearty and zealous service.

His powers were exerted with care and skill unmarred by impulse, temper, or vacillation. His mind was a vast storehouse of details, historical, biographical, descriptive, bearing on the whole political relations of the nations of Europe, and the position of this country in regard to them; coupled with the most profound and extensive knowledge of men and manners, the springs of human action, the motives to sway men's judgment. No one ever heard Lord Palmerston as the *Laudator temporis acti*. He had no feeble allusions to former triumphs, nor complacent recallings of the great deeds of yore. One could not tell, save from the striking maturity of his views and the firmness of his conclusions, that his experience had been greater than that of his audience. That which showed the true power of his mind was the lucid, well-balanced, rapid grasp with which he apprehended the question immediately to hand, shutting out entirely all others, and bringing to bear on the topic before him all the resources of his knowledge.

A happy temperament, kindly humour, good breeding, and unfailing health made Lord Palmerston friends wherever he went, but the true source of the unbounded confidence with which the nation regarded him was the calm, unimpassioned, weighty power by which his political acts and opinions were distinguished. He loved his country and his country loved him. He lived for her honour, and she will cherish his memory.